D1559403

ANTHONY TROLLOPE
A Collector's Catalogue
1847 – 1990

ANTHONY TROLLOPE
A Collector's Catalogue
1847 – 1990

The Trollope Society
London
1992

This work has been partly based, with permission, on *The Trollope Collector* (1985)
by Lance Tingay
© 1992: The Trollope Society

ISBN 1 870587 98 7

Printed and bound in Great Britain by
Butler & Tanner Ltd, Frome and London

PREFACE

Part One of this list of works by and about Anthony Trollope is based on Lance Tingay's *The Trollope Collector* (1985) which is reprinted here with the twin aims of providing the reader of Trollope with a useful working tool and of celebrating Tingay's long and valuable contribution to Trollope studies.

Trollope's readers have long been fortunate in having Michael Sadleir's excellent and detailed bibliography of the early editions. First published in 1928, and supplemented with corrections in 1934, it became so much a model of how such work should be carried out that some people attribute the subsequent collectability of Trollope first editions to Sadleir's meticulous accuracy. Tingay's work, with its immense range and detail, covering translations, reprints and adaptations up to the present day, should be seen as complimenting Sadleir's book. In this edition it has been updated and added to, but its characteristic flavour and occasional eccentricity have been retained.

Part Two consists of a list of books and articles about Trollope, from the reviews of his first novel, *The Macdermots of Ballycloran* (1847) up to 1990. For reviews published in Trollope's lifetime the compilers have leaned heavily on David Skilton's *Anthony Trollope and his contemporaries* (1972), but we believe this to be the first comprehensive listing of reviews arranged by order of the novels' first publication. Mary Leslie Irwin's *Anthony Trollope, a bibliography* (1926) has also been useful for works published up to 1925, and *The Reputation of Anthony Trollope* by Olmsted and Welch (1978) is invaluable for modern times. As explained in the note to Part Two, no attempt has been made to be comprehensive for the years 1885-1975, and only the principal books and articles on Trollope, or those contributing significant new information have been included. For the years 1976 to 1990, all published articles and books on Trollope, as well as reviews of works about him have been listed. It is hoped that this section will be supplemented annually in *Trollopiana* to provide a frequently-updated bibliography for students of Trollope.

This revision of Tingay's work has been undertaken by David Skilton, Claire Connolly and Christopher Edwards.

PART ONE
Published works by Anthony Trollope
Originally published as **The Trollope Collector** *by Lance Tingay, Silverbridge Press 1985.*

Section A: Separate titles

1. THE MACDERMOTS OF BALLYCLORAN

Written: autumn 1843-1845.
Book publication:
1847   L: Newby, 3 vols; re-issued 1848.
1861   L: Chapman & Hall; Standard Library
1865   Select Library of Fiction no 86 1866; 4th edn 1867; 5th edn. 1869; 6th edn. 1871.*
1870   Philadelphia: Peterson.*
1871   L/NY: Routledge.*
1880   L: Ward Lock, Select Library of Fiction no 2.*
1882   NY: Munro, Seaside Library.*
1894   NY: Lupton.*
1906   L/NY: Lane, New Pocket Library, intro Algar Thorold.*
1979   NY: Garland, 3 vols.
1981   NY: Arno Press, 3 vols, intro N. John Hall.
(*Lacking chapters II, III and XII of volume 3 of the original Newby edn.)
1988   NY: Dover Publications
1989   L: OUP World's Classics, ed Robert Tracy.
1991   L: Trollope Society, intro O. Dudley Edwards. Folio Society, as above, ill Elisa Trimby.

2. THE KELLYS AND THE O'KELLYS

Written: 1847.
Book publication:
1848   L: Colburn, 3 vols.
1859   L: Chapman & Hall; 3rd Edn 1860; 4th Edn 1861, 5th Edn 1865; Select Library of Fiction no 93 1866; 6th Edn 1867, 8th Edn 1868; 9th Edn 1870; 10th Edn 1872; 1874. NY: Rudd & Carleton.
1871   L/NY: Routledge.
1880   L: Ward Lock, Select Library of Fiction no 4.
1882   NY: Munro, Seaside Library.
1906   L/NY: Lane, New Pocket Library, intro Algar Thorold.
1929   L/NY: OUP World's Classics no 341; reprinted 1978.
1937   NY: Random House, intro Shane Leslie.
1979   NY: Garland, 3 vols, intro Robert Lee Wolff.
1982   L: OUP World's Classics, ed W.J. McCormack, intro William Trevor.

3. LA VENDÉE

Written: 1849
Book Publication:
1850   L: Colburn, 3 vols; reissued same year.
1874   L: Chapman & Hall, Select Library of Fiction no 242*; 4th Edn 1875; 1878.
1880   L: Ward Lock, Select Library of Fiction no 13.
1981   NY: Arno Press, 3 vols, intro Robert Tracy.
(* A brief footnote was added by A.T. in 1874.)

4. THE WARDEN

Written: 29 July 1853 - autumn 1854.
Serialised: L'Union Liberale [Neuchâtel] 1879 (French - **Legs de John Hiram**, trans Charles Berthoud).
Book publication:
1855   L: Longman; further edns 1858, 1859, 1866, 1870, 1877, 1878, 1886, 1894, 1902.
1859   Leipzig: Tauchnitz.
1862   NY: Dick & Fitzgerald, Hand & Pocket Library.
1870   NY: Harper, Library of Select Novels no 351 (with **Barchester Towers**). Philadelphia: Lippincott.
1878   L: Chapman & Hall, vol 1 of **The Chronicles of Barsetshire**, with chapters 1-18 of **Barchester Towers** and with preface to series by A.T., fp F.A. Fraser; further issues 1887, 1891.
1879   Neuchâtel: Sandoz & Fischbacher (French - **Le Guardien**, trans Charles Berthoud).
1885   NY: Munro, Seaside Library, pocket edn.
1892   NY: Dodd, Mead, with A.T.'s preface to Barset series; further issues 1898, 1902, 1903, 1927, 1930.
1900   Philadelphia: Gebbie, Collector's Edn vol 1, with biography of A.T. and intro H.T. Peck.
1902   L/NY: Lane, New Pocket Library, intro Algar Thorold.
1904   L: Routledge / NY: Dutton, ill F.C. Tilney; further issue 1908.
1906   L: Bell / NY: Macmillan [1907], with intro toBarset series by Frederic Harrison; further issues 1910, 1923, 1924, 1926; in Bohn's Popular Library 1913, 1923, 1928.
1907   L: Dent / NY: Dutton, Everyman's Library no 182, intro Ernest Rhys; reprinted 1910, 1912, 1916, 1920, 1926, 1929, 1936, 1941,

1944, 1953; intro Kathleen Tillotson 1958, 1961, 1963, 1969.
NY: Longman.

1914　L: Nelson, New Century Library; also in 1 vol with **Doctor Thorne**; in Nelson's Classics 1929, 1954; intro John Hampden 1956.

[1917?]　L: Richard Butterworth.

1918　L/NY: OUP World's Classics no 217; reprinted 1928, 1932, 1939, 1942, 1949, 1950, 1955, 1958; intro Richard Church 1961, 1963 (twice), 1966, 1968.

1925　L: Harrap, Standard Fiction Library; reprinted 1929.
L: Hayes, ill F.C. Tilney.
NY: Dial Press.
NY: Harcourt.

1926　L: Mathews & Marrot, ill E. Gabain.
NY: Macmillan, Macmillan's Pocket Classics, ed Jessie du val Myers.
Boston: Lauriat.

[1927?]　L: Waverley, ill F.C. Tilney.

1928　L: Lane.

1929　Oxford: Blackwell, Shakespeare Head Press, intro to Barset series Michael Sadleir / Boston: Houghton Mifflin 1931.

1931　NY: Book League of America.

1932　NY: Pratt Institute Library, ed E.F. Stevens.

1935　NY: Doubleday Doran, ed and intro R.M. Gay

1936　NY: Modern Library / L: Hamish Hamilton 1937, with **Barchester Towers**, intro A. Edward Newton; further issue 1946; intro Harlan Hatcher 1950.

1944　L: Penguin Books; further issues 1945, 1982; intro Robin Gilmour 1984.

1946　Bognor, England: Crowther, rewritten for children H. Oldfield Box.
Brussels: Editions la Boetie (French - **Le Directeur**, trans J. Staquet).
L: Chatto & Windus, Zodiac Press; further issues 1949, 1953, 1962, 1967, 1973, 1978, 1982 / NY: Grove Press 1952 / Harcourt 1962.

1947　L: Mellifont Press, abridged.
Paris: Nouvelles Editions Latines (French - **La Sinecure**).

1948　NY: Dodd, Mead, abridged and with **Barchester Towers**, intro Marion E. Dodd.

1949　L: Harrap, ill Phyllis Harrap.

1950　L: Classics Book Club.
L: OUP English Readers Library, abridged and ed Lord Hemingford, ill A.E. Batchelor; reprinted 1952, 1956, 1959, 1960, 1961.
NY: Doric Books, ill Paul Crowley.

1951　Milan: Garmanti (Italian - **Un Caso di Coscienza**, trans and preface A. Lombardo).

1952　L/NY/Toronto: OUP The Oxford Trollope, ill Edward Ardizzone, intro to Barset series Ronald Knox; reprinted 1952.

Milan: Rizzoli (Italian - **Gli Scrupoli Mister Harding**, trans L. Berti).

1953　Helsinki: Werner Soderstrom (Finnish **Vanhen Miehen Omatunte**).

1955　L: Collins, intro A.O.J. Cockshut; reprinted 1960, 1963.
L: Dent, Literature of Today & Yesterday; reprinted 1957.
L: Heinemann, Guide Novel Series, ed N.L. Clay.
NY: Limited Editions Club / Heritage Press, intro Angela Thirkell, ill Fritz Kredel.

[1959?]　Peking: Chinese translation.

1960　NY: Doubleday Doran, Dolphin Books.

1961　L: Icon Books.
L: Longman, intro and notes Anthea Bell.

1962　NY: Washington Square Press, intro Bradford A. Booth.

1964　NY: New American Library, Signet Classics, afterword Geoffrey Tillotson.

1966　Boston: Houghton Mifflin, Riverside Edn, with **Barchester Towers**, intro L. Auchincloss.
Oslo: De Unges Forlag (Norwegian - **Pastor Harding Samvittighet**).

1967　L: University of London Press, intro and notes G.C. Rosser.

1968　NY: Lance Books.

1976　L: Folio Society, intro Julian Symons, ill Peter Reddick.

1980　L: OUP World's Classics, intro and notes David Skilton, ill Edward Ardizzone.

1984　L: Penguin, English Library.

5. BARCHESTER TOWERS

Written: April 1855 - November 1856.
Book Publication:

1857　L: Longman, 3 vols; in 1 vol People's Edition 1858; further editions 1859, 1861, 1866, 1870, 1876, 1886, 1891, 1900, 1903.

1859　Leipzig: Tauchnitz, 2 vols.

1860　NY: Dick & Fitzgerald, 2 vols & 1 vol; Hand & Pocket Library 1862.

1870　Philadelphia: Lippincott.
NY: Harper, Library of Select Novels no 351 (with **The Warden**).

1878/79　L: Chapman & Hall, 2 vols, the first containing **The Warden** and Chapters 1-18 of **Barchester Towers**, being vols 1/2 of **The Chronicles of Barsetshire**, fp F.A. Fraser; further issues 1887, 1891.

1881　NY: Munro, Seaside Library.

1886　Paris: Hachette, 2 vols (French - **Les Tours de Barchester**, trans L. Bartel).

1892　NY: Dodd, Mead, 2 vols, fp by C.R. Grant; further issues 1904, 1908, 1922, 1927.

1900　Philadelphia: Gebbie, Collector's Edn vols 2/3.

1902 L/NY: Lane, New Pocket Library; further issue 1914.
NY: Century Co., The English Comedie Humaine Series, ill Hugh M. Eaton; reprinted 1903, 1904, 1906.

1903 L: Blackie, ill L.L. Brooke; further issue 1931; in Great Novelists Library 1932.

1904 L: Routledge / NY: Dutton, ill F.C. Tilney; further issue 1909.

1906 L: Dent / NY: Dutton, ill Everyman's Library no 30, intro Ernest Rhys; reprinted same year, 1909, 1912, 1915, 1920, 1923, 1926, 1929, 1931, 1936, 1938, 1945,1949; with intro Michael Sadleir 1956, 1962, 1969.
L: Bell / NY: Macmillan [1907]; further issues 1909, 1910, 1914, 1920, 1923, 1924, 1926, 1928; in Bohn's Popular Library 1913.

1908 NY: Longman.
Philadelphia: Winston.
L: Collins, Illustrated Pocket Classics, ill Paul Hardy; Canterbury Classics 1939.

1909 L: Cassell, People's Library / NY: Funk & Wagnall.

1913 L: Nelson, New Century Library, ill Heber Thompson; Nelson's Classics 1917, 1923, 1954, 1959; Famous Books Series 1932.

1923 NY: Scribners Modern Student's Library, intro C.B. Stevens.

1924 L: Gresham Publishing Co., intro W.K. Leask, ill L.L. Brooke.

1925 L/NY: OUP World's Classics no 268; reprinted 1928, 1932, 1935, 1939, 1941, 1942, 1947, 1949, 1951; with intro R.H. Taylor 1960, 1962, 1966.
L: Hayes, ill F.C. Tilney.
NY: Harcourt.

1926 Boston: Lauriat.
NY: Macmillan, Macmillan's Readers Series, intro J.I. Osborne; reprinted 1929, 1930, 1938.

[1927?] L: Waverley, ill F.C. Tilney.

1928 L: Lane; reprinted 1939, 1945.

1929 Oxford: Blackwell, Shakespeare Head Press, 2 vols.

1931 L: Odhams Press.

1936 NY: Modern Library / L: Hamish Hamilton [1937], with The Warden, intro A. Edward Newton; reprinted 1946; with intro Harlan Hatcher 1950.

1941 L: Dent, Literature of Yesterday and Today; reprinted 1948.
L: Classics Book Club, 2 vols.

1945 NY: Doubleday Doran, ill Donald Mckay.

1946 L: Collins, Laurel & Gold Series, abridged.
L: Chatto & Windus, Zodiac Press; reprinted 1949, 1952, 1958, 1962, 1967, 975 / NY: Grove Press 1952 / NY: Harcourt 1962.
L: Pilot Press, in Novels and Stories (see item A94); reprinted 1947, 1949.

1947 L: Percy Press; reprinted 1948.

Stockholm: Saxon & Lindstrom (Swedish - Biskopen i Barchester, trans Harald Jernstrom).

1948 NY: Dodd, Mead, abridged, with The Warden, intro Marion E. Dodd.
L: Todd, Modern Reading Library, / Canada: Clarke Irwin, abridged.

1949 L: Nicholas Vane.
NY: Rhinehart, intro Bradford A. Booth; reprinted 1957, 1960, 1961.

1951 Oslo: Mortensens, 2 vols (Norwegian - Det Hendte i Barchester).
Lublijana: Drzavne Zalozba Sloveniji (Slovene - Pod Zvoniki Barchestra, trans Izidor Cankar.)

1952 L: Hodder & Stoughton, abridged with intro by H. Oldfield Box.
L: Collins, intro Pamela Hansford Johnson; reprinted 1961, 1966, 1975.
Cleveland, Ohio: Fine Editions Press, intro William Targ.
Milan: Garzani (Italian - I Torri di Barchester, trans Agostino Lombardo).

1953 L/NY/Toronto: OUP The Oxford Trollope, 2 vols, ed Michael Sadleir & Frederick Page, notes by R.W. Chapman, ill Edward Ardizzone.

1956 L: Thames, abridged.
Turin: Unione Tipografica Editrice Torinese, 2 vols (Italian - I Torri di Barchester, trans., notes, intro Vittoria Sanna).

1957 L: Penguin Books; reprinted 1982; in English Library, intro & notes Robin Gilmour, preface J.K. Galbraith, 1983.

1958 NY: Limited Editions Club / Heritage Press, intro Angela Thirkell, ill Fritz Kredel.

1959 NY: Bantam Books.

1962 NY: Doubleday Doran, Dolphin Books.

1963 L: Longman, abridged and ed Barry Taylor, ill Victor Ambrus.
NY: Signet Classics, afterword Robert W. Daniel.
NY: Washington Square Press, intro R.H. Singleton.

1966 L: Dean & Son, Classics Series, abridged.
Boston: Houghton Mifflin, Riverside Edn, with The Warden, intro L. Auchincloss.

[1966?] L: Heron books, intro R.H. Taylor (from the World's Classics 1960 edn), ill Edward Ardizzone (from the 1953 Oxford Trollope).

1970 Moscow (Russian - Barchesrskec Bamne).

1974 NY/ L: Peebles Classics Library, 2 vols.

1977 L: Folio Society, intro Julian Symons, ill Peter Reddick.

1980 L: OUP World's Classics, ed Michael Sadleir & Frederick Page, notes R.W. Chapman, ill Edward Ardizzone (as in the Oxford Trollope edn 1953), intro James R. Kincaid; issued also as hardback.
L: Pan Books, intro & notes David Skilton.

8

6. THE THREE CLERKS

Written: Spring - 18 August 1857.
Book publication:

1858   L: Bentley, Standard Novels 3 vols* [issued Nov 1857]; in 1 vol 1859, 1860, 1861, 1865, 1866, 1872, 1874, 1878, 1883, 1890, 1891.
1860   NY: Harper; further issue 1874.
1874   Berlin: Engelmann, Asher's Library, 2 vols.
1886   NY: Munro, Seaside Library, pocket edn.
1900   L: Macmillan.
1903   L: Long, Library of Modern Classics, intro Hannaford Bennett, ill P.B. Hickling.
1904   L/NY: Lane, New Pocket Library, intro Algar Thorold.
1907   L: OUP World's Classics no 140, intro W. Teignmouth Shore; reprinted 1925, 1929, 1943, 1952, 1959, 1978.
1932   L: Longman, Simplified English Series, ed A.L. Walker, ill Daphne B. Rowles.
1958   Israel: Hebrew translation.
1981   NY: Dover Publications.
      NY: Arno, 3 vols, intro Asa Briggs.
1986   Gloucester, England: Alan Sutton.
(* Chapter XII of vol 2 of the 1st edn was subsequently omitted.)

7. DOCTOR THORNE

Written: 20 October 1857 - 1 April 1858.
Serialised: La Revue Britannique, Jan-Nov 1863 (French).
Book publication:

1858   L: Chapman & Hall, 3 vols; 2nd edn same year; in 1 vol Standard Novels 1859 (twice), 4th edn 1860, 1861, 7th edn 1862, 1864; in Select Library of Fiction no 85 1865, 1866, 1867, 1868, 1873, 1882.
      NY: Harper; in Library of Select Novels no 416 1874.
      Leipzig: Tauchnitz, 2 vols.
1860   Amsterdam: Ringer, 3 vols (Dutch - **De Doctor**, trans Mevr van Westerheene).
1861   Copenhagen: Jordan, 3 vols (Danish - **Doctor Thorne**).
1863   Naumburg, Germany: Patz, 5 vols (French - **Le Docteur Thorne**).
      Paris: Bibliothèque Choisie (French - **Le Docteur Thorne**).
      Wurzen: Verlags-Comptoir, 6 vols (German **Doctor Thorne**, trans A. Kretzschmar)
1864   Paris: Bureau de la Revue Britannique (French - **Le Doctor Thorne**).
1866   NY: Appleton.
1871   L/NY: Routledge.
1879   L: Chapman & Hall, fp F.A. Fraser, vol 3 of **The Chronicles of Barsetshire**; further issues 1887, 1893.
1880   L: Ward Lock, Select Library of Fiction no 1.

1882   NY: Munro, Seaside Library, 2 parts.
1892   NY: Dodd, Mead, 2 vols; further issue 1903.
1900   Philadelphia: Gebbie, 2 vols, Collector's Edition vols 4, 5.
1902   L/NY: Lane, New Pocket Library, intro Algar Thorold.
1906   L: Bell / NY: Macmillan [1907]; further issues 1923, 1926, 1928; in Bohn's Popular Library 1914.
1909   L: Routledge / NY: Dutton, ill H.L. Shindler.
      L: Dent / NY: Dutton, Everyman's Library no 360, intro Ernest Rhys; reprinted 1915, 1930, 1936, 1949, 1953, 1967.
1914   L: Nelson, New Century Library; and in 1 vol with **The Warden**; in Nelson's Classics 1952.
1924   L: Bell / NY: Harcourt [1925].
1925   L: Hayes, ill H.L. Shindler.
1926   Boston: Lauriat.
      L/NY: OUP World's Classics no 298; reprinted 1934, 1941, 1943, 1947, 1951, 1953, 1956, 1963, 1966.
[1927?]   L: Waverley, ill H.L. Shindler.
1928   L: Lane.
1929   Oxford: Blackwell, Shakespeare Head Press, 2 vols.
1947   L: Chatto & Windus, Zodiac Press; reprinted 1962, 1967 / NY: Grove Press 1952 / NY: Harcourt 1962.
1949   L: Dent, Literature of Today & Yesterday.
1951-2   Oslo: Mortensens, 2 vols. (Norwegian - **Doktor Thorne**, trans Othar Berthung).
1954   Zurich: Manessa Verlag (German - **Doktor Thorne**, with postscript by Max Wildi).
1957   L: Longman, written within vocabulary of New Reader 4 by Michael West & E.P. Hart, ill Monica Goddard.
1959   Cambridge, Mass: Riverside Library, intro Elizabeth Bowen; reprinted in her **Afterthought** (L: Longman 1962) pp 13-39 and her **Seven Winters & Afterthought** (NY: Knopf 1962) pp 96-130.
1961   NY: Doubleday Doran, Dolphin Books.
1968   L: Pan Books, intro Julian Symons, notes Arthur Calder-Marshall.
1978   L: Folio Society, intro Julian Symons, ill Peter Reddick.
1980   L: OUP World's Classics, intro David Skilton.
1991   L: Penguin Classics, ed Ruth Rendell.

8. THE BERTRAMS

Written: 1 April - 20 December 1858.
Serialised: Revue Nationale, Apr-Oct 1864 (French - **Bertrams**). 16 years after book publication in the Manchester Weekly Times Supplement, 30 Jan 1876 - 9 Jun 1877.
Book Publication:

1859	L: Chapman & Hall, 3 vols. 2nd edn 1859; in 1 vol 1860, 4th edn 1861, 1862; Select Library of Fiction no 100 1866, 1867, 1868, 1869. NY: Harper; reprinted 1866, 1871; Franklin Square Library no 85 1879. Leipzig: Tauchnitz, 2 vols.	
1859-60	Wurzen: Verlags-Comptoir, 6 vols (German - **Die Bertrams**, trans A. Kretzchmar).	
1860	Sneed: Van Druten und Blecker, 2 vols (Dutch - **De Bertrams**).	
1863	Denmark: Jordan, 3 vols (Danish - **Familien Bertram**).	
1866	Paris: Charpentier, 2 vols (French - **Les Bertrams**).	
1871	L/NY: Routledge.	
1880	L: Ward Lock, Select Library of Fiction no 7.	
1905	L/NY: Lane, New Pocket Library, intro Algar Thorold.	
1981	NY: Arno, 3 vols, intro James R. Kincaid.	
1986	Gloucester England: Alan Sutton intro Sheila Mitchell.	
1987	NY: Dover Publications.	
1991	L: OUP World's Classics, ed Geoffrey Harvey.	

9. THE WEST INDIES AND THE SPANISH MAIN

Written: February - summer 1859.
Serialised: Bibliothèque Universelle et Revue Suisse, 1863, vol 16: 464-96, 628-63, excerpts trans into French by L. Etienne.
Book Publication:

1859	L: Chapman & Hall; further editions 1860 (twice), 1862, 1866, 1867, 1869.
1860	NY: Harper: further edn 1872. Leipzig: Tauchnitz.
1925	San Jose, Costa Rica: Publication of the Lyceum of Costa Rica, series A: no 12 (Spanish - **Las Indias y el Continenta Espanol**, translation by R. Fernandez of chapters 17-20).
1968	L: Cass/NY: Barnes & Noble. L: Dawson.
1985	Gloucester, England : Alan Sutton/NY: Hippodrome Books intro Sheila Mitchell.

10. CASTLE RICHMOND

Written: 4 August 1859 - 31 March 1860.
Serialised: La Revue Britannique, Jan-Nov 1861 (French).
Book publication:

1860	L: Chapman & Hall, 3 vols; in 1 vol 1861, 1862; Select Library of Fiction no 96 1866, 4th edn 1867, 1870 (8th edn), 1877.

	NY: Harper. Leipzig: Tauchnitz, 2 vols. Denmark: Pio, 2 vols (Danish - **Castle Richmond**). Wurzen: Verlags-Comptoir, 6 vols (German - **Schloss Richmond**, trans A. Kretzschmar).
1862	Amsterdam: Syrbandi, 2 vols (Dutch - **Het Kasteel Richmond**).
1863	Naumburg: Patz, 5 vols (French - **Chateau Richmond**).
1871	L/NY: Routledge.
1880	L: Ward Lock, Select Library of Fiction no 6.
1882	NY: Munro, Seaside Library.
1906	L/NY: Lane, New Pocket Library, intro Algar Thorold.
1979	NY: Garland, 3 vols.
1981	NY: Arno Press, 3 vols, intro Janet Egleson Dunleavy.
1984	NY: Dover Publications.
1989	L: OUP World's Classics, ed Mary Hamer.

11. FRAMLEY PARSONAGE

Written: 4 November 1859 - 30 June 1860.
MS: Harrow School, London (Vaughan Library). Lacks ch 1-18.
Serialisation: Cornhill, Jan 1860-Apr 1861, vols 1-3 (anonymously).
Book Publication:

1861	L: Smith, Elder, 3 vols, ill Millais; in 1 vol 1861, 1862, 1866, 1869, 1872, 1876, 1878, 1886, 1890, 1896, 1906. NY: Harper; further issue 1873; Franklin Square Library no 73 1879. Leipzig: Tauchnitz, 2 vols. St Petersburg: (Russian - **Fremlyeejski Prijkhod**).
1864	Wurzen: Verlags-Comptoir, 6 vols (German - **Das Pfarrhaus Framley**, trans A. Kretzchmar); further issue 1867.
1879	L: Chapman & Hall, vol 4 of **The Chronicles of Barsetshire**, fp F.A. Fraser; further issues 1887, 1891.
1884	NY: Munro, Seaside Library.
1892	NY: Dodd, Mead, 2 vols; further issue 1903.
1900	Philadelphia: Gebbie, 2 vols, Collector's Edition vols 6-7.
1903	L/NY: Lane, New Pocket Library.
1904	L: Blackie, ill C.A. Shepperson.
1906	L: Bell / NY: Macmillan [1907]; further issues 1923, 1926, 1928; Bohn's Popular Library 1914. L: Dent / NY: Dutton, Everyman's Library no 181, intro Ernest Rhys; reprinted 1910, 1912, 1932; intro Kathleen Tillotson 1961, 1966.
1908	L: Collins, ill Ray Potter; reprinted 1929.
1909	L: Routledge / NY: Dutton, ill Millais.

Philadelphia: Winston.
1914 L: Nelson, New Century Library; Nelson's
Classics 1925; intro Sir Arthur Quiller-
Couch 1954, 1955.
1924 L: Bell / NY: Harcourt [1925].
1925 L: Hayes, ill Millais.
1926 L/NY: OUP World's Classics no 305;
reprinted 1939, 1944, 1950, 1951, 1961.
Boston: Lauriat.
[1927?] L: Waverley, ill Millais.
1928 L: Lane.
1929 Oxford: Blackwell, Shakespeare Head
Press, 2 vols.
1941 L: Classics Book Club.
1947 L: Harrap, Holborn Library, intro S.E.B.
L: Chatto & Windus, Zodiac Press;
reprinted 1950, 1955, 1962, 1972 / NY:
Grove Press 1952 / NY: Harcourt 1962.
1952 Oslo: Mortensens, 2 vols (Norwegian -
Prestegarden i Framley).
1978 L: Folio Society, intro Julian Symons, ill
Peter Reddick.
1980 L: OUP World's Classics, intro P.D.
Edwards.
1984 L: Penguin Books, ed David Skilton & Peter
Miles.
1989 NY: OUP

12. TALES OF ALL COUNTRIES [1st Series]

Comprising *La Mère Bauche, The O'Conors of Castle
Conor, John Bull on the Guadalquivir, Miss Sarah
Jack of Spanish Town Jamaica, The Courtship of
Susan Bell, Relics of General Chasse, An Unprotected
Female at the Pyramids, The Chateau of Prince
Polignac.*

Book Publication:
1861 L: Chapman & Hall.
1931 L/NY: OUP World's Classics, no 397.
1981 NY: Arno Press, intro Jane Egleson
Dunleavy.

13. ORLEY FARM

Written: 4 July 1860 - 15 June 1861.
MS: Princeton University, Princeton, New Jersey
(Taylor Collection).
Part issue: 20 monthly parts, Mar 1861 - Oct 1862
(L: Chapman & Hall).
Serialised: Harper's Magazine, May 1861 - Dec
1862, vols 22-26.
Revue Nationale Mar 1865 - Aug 1866 (French - **Le
Ferme d'Orley**).
Book publication:
1861-62 L: Chapman & Hall, 2 vols, ill Millais; in 1
vol Select Library of Fiction no 116 1868,
1871, 5th edn.

1862 NY: Harper, ill Millais.
Leipzig: Tauchnitz, 3 vols.
1864 Amsterdam: Syrbandi, 2 vols (Dutch - **De
Aanklegt van Meineed**).
St Petersburg: (Russian - **Orleysaskaya
Fyerma**).
Wurzen: Verlags-Comptoir, 5 vols (German
- **Orley Farm**, trans A. Kretzchmar).
1865 Leipzig: Gunther, 6 vols (German - **Orley
Farm**, trans C. Markgraff).
1871 L/NY: Routledge. (reissue of 1st edn in 1
vol, with new title page).
1880 L: Ward Lock, Select Library of Fiction no
22; New Standard Library no. 191 same
year.
1882 NY: Munro, Seaside Library, 2 parts.
1905 NY: Dodd, Mead, 3 vols.
1906 L: Lane, New Pocket Library, 2 vols. intro
Algar Thorold.
1910 L: Collins, Illustrated Pocket Classics, ill
F.C. Tilney.
1935 L/NY: OUP World's Classics, 2 vols, nos.
423, 424; also 1 vol; reprinted 1 vol 1951,
1956, 1963, 1970.
1950 NY: Knopf, intro Henry S. Drinker.
1951 L: Hodder & Stoughton, abridged and intro
H. Oldfield Box.
1981 NY: Dover Publications, ill Millais.
1985 L: OUP World's Classics.

14. THE STRUGGLES OF BROWN, JONES AND ROBINSON

Written: July 1857 - 3 August 1861.
Serialised: Cornhill, Aug 1861-March 1862, vols 4-5.
Book Publication:
1862 NY: Harper, Library of Select Novels no
220.
1870 L: Smith, Elder, Popular Works; further
issue 1876.
1882 NY: Munro, Seaside Library.
1981 NY: Arno Press, intro N. John Hall.

15. NORTH AMERICA

Written: 16 September 1861 - April 1862.
MS: E. Joseph Booksellers, London (1991).
Book publication:
1862 L: Chapman & Hall, 2 vols; 2nd and 3rd
editions same year; 1864; in 1 vol 1866,
1868.
NY: Harper; reprinted 1871-76.
Philadelphia: Lippincott, 2 vols.
Leipzig: Tauchnitz, 3 vols.
Leipzig: Tauchnitz, 3 vols (German - **Nord-
America**, trans A. Diezmann).
1951 NY: Knopf, intro Bradford A. Booth &
Donald A. Smalley.

1968	L: Dawson, 2 vols.
	L: Penguin Books, ed Robert Mason, intro
	John William Ward (a shortened version).
1986	NY: Da Capo Press
1986	L: Publications, 2 vols.
1987	Gloucester, England: Alan Sutton, 2 vols.

16. TALES OF ALL COUNTRIES, SECOND SERIES

Comprising *Aaron Trow, Mrs General Talboys, The Parson's Daughter of Oxney Colne, George Walker at Suez, The Mistletoe Bough, Returning Home, A Ride across Palestine, The House of the Heine Brothers at Munich, The Man who Kept his Money in a Box.*
Book publication:
1863   L: Chapman & Hall. For subsequent editions see below, no 17.
1981   NY: Arno Press, intro Donald D. Stone.

17. TALES OF ALL COUNTRIES

Comprising 1st and 2nd Series.
Book publication:
1863   L: Chapman & Hall; further issue 1864; Select Library of Fiction no 95 1866, 1867, 1871, 1873, 1877.
1871   L/NY: Routledge.
1880   L: Ward Lock, Select Library of Fiction no 5.

18. RACHEL RAY

Written: 3 March - 29 June 1863.
MS: New York Public Library, New York (Arents Collection).
Book publication:
1863   L: Chapman & Hall, 2 vols; 4th edn same year; 6th edn 1864; in 1 vol with fp by Millais 1864; Select Library of Fiction no 88 1866,1867 (9th edn),1869, 1871 (12th edn).
NY: Harper, Library of Select Novels no 237.
Leipzig: Tauchnitz, 2 vols.
1864   St Petersburg: (Russian - **Rachel Ray**).
1871   L/NY: Routledge.
1880   L: Ward Lock, Select Library of Fiction no 3.
1884   NY: Munro, Seaside Library.
1869   Paris: Hachette, 2 vols (French - **Rachel Ray**, trans L. Martel).
1906   L/NY: Lane, New Pocket Library, intro Algar Thorold.
1924   L: OUP World's Classics no 279.
1952   NY: Knopf, intro B.R. Redman.
1980   NY: Dover Publications.
1981   NY: Arno, 2 vols, intro Andrew Wright.

1988	L: OUP World's Classics.
1990	L: Trollope Society, intro John Letts.
	L: Folio Society: as above, ill David Eccles.

19. THE CIVIL SERVICE AS A PROFESSION

Written: 1861-3
Book publication:
[1861-3]? Privately printed for A.T., 36pp pamphlet.
1938   L: Constable, ed and intro Morris L. Parrish, limited to 150 copies. With three other lectures (items A20, A38 and A42).
1976   Philadelphia: Folcroft.

20. THE PRESENT CONDITION OF THE NORTHERN STATES OF THE AMERICAN UNION

Written: late 1862 or 1863.
Book publication:
[1861-3]? Privately printed for A.T., 32pp pamphlet.
1938   L: Constable, ed and intro Morris L. Parrish, limited to 150 copies. With three other lectures (items A19, A38 and A42).
1976   Philadelphia: Folcroft.

21. THE SMALL HOUSE AT ALLINGTON

Written: 20 May 1862 - 11 February 1863.
MS: Huntington Library, San Marino, California.
Serialised: Cornhill, Sep 1862-Apr 1864, vols 6-9 (anonymously until vol 9); Harper's Magazine, Dec 1862-Jun 1864, vols 25-29.
Book publication:
1864   L: Smith, Elder, 2 vols, ill Millais; reprinted twice same year; in 1 vol 1864, 1869, 1872, 1876, 1885, 1894, 1902, 1903.
NY: Harper.
Leipzig: Tauchnitz, 3 vols.
St Petersburg: 2 vols (Russian - **Allingtonskey Maliy Dom**).
1866   Paris: Lacroix Verboeckhoven, 2 vols (French - **La Petite Maison d'Allington**).
1879   L: Chapman & Hall, 2 vols, vols. 4-5 of **The Chronicles of Barsetshire**, fp F.A. Fraser, further issues 1884, 1893.
1883   NY: Munro, Seaside Library, 2 parts.
1892   NY: Dodd, Mead, 3 vols; further issues 1904, 1927.
1900   Philadelphia: Gebbie, 3 vols, Collector's Edition vols 8-9-10.
1906   L: Lane, New Pocket Library, 2 vols, intro Algar Thorold.
1906   L: Bell / NY: Macmillan [1907], 2 vols; further issues 1913, 1923, 1924, 1926, 1928; in Bohn's Popular Library 1914.
1909   L: Dent / NY: Dutton, Everyman's Library

no 361; reprinted 1910, 1915, 1923, 1928, 1934, 1963, 1965.
L: Routledge / NY: Dutton, ill Millais.
1914　L: Nelson, New Century Library; Nelson's Classics 1948.
1925　L: Hayes, ill Millais.
1926　Boston: Lauriat.
[1927?]　L: Waverley, ill Millais.
1928　L: Lane, 2 vols.
1929　Oxford: Blackwell, Shakespeare Head Press, 2 vols.
1939　L/NY: OUP World's Classics, 2 vols, nos.472-473; in 1 vol 1950, 1959, 1963.
1948　L: Chatto & Windus, Zodiac Press; reprinted 1950, 1972 / NY: Grove Press 1952 / NY: Harcourt 1962.
1950　L: Dent, Literature of Today & Yesterday.
1952　Oslo: Mortensens, 2 vols (Norwegian - **Sostene i Allington**).
1979　L: Folio Society, intro Julian Symons, ill Peter Reddick.
1980　L: OUP World's Classics, intro J.R. Kincaid.
1989　N.Y: OUP ed J.R. Kincaid.
1991　L: Penguin Classics, ed Julian Thompson.

22. CAN YOU FORGIVE HER?

Written: 16 August 1863 - 28 April 1864.
MS: Yale University, New Haven, Connecticut (Beinecke Library).
Part issue: 20 monthly parts, Jan 1864-Aug 1865 (L: Chapman & Hall).
Book publication:
1864-65 L: Chapman & Hall, 2 vols, ill Phiz & Miss Taylor; in 1 vol 1866; 2 vols bound in 1 (3rd edn); 1871, 2 vols in 1 (5th edn). Select Library of Fiction no 120 1868, 1875.
1865　NY: Harper. Leipzig: Tauchnitz, 3 vols.
1866　Denmark: Jordan, 3 vols (Danish - **Kan Tilgive Hende ?**).
1867　Amsterdam: Syrbandi, 3 vols (Dutch - **Kunt Gij't Haar Vergeven?**).
1871　L/NY: Routledge.
1880　L: Ward Lock, Select Library of Fiction no 23; reprinted 1889.
1893　NY: Dodd, Mead, 3 vols; further issue 1900 1903.
1900　Philadelphia: Gebbie, 3 vols, Collector's Edition vols 14-16.
1906　L/NY: Lane, New Pocket Library, 2 vols.
1938　L/NY: OUP World's Classics, 2 vols, nos. 468-469; and in 1 vol; reprinted 1958, 1963.
1948　L/NY/Toronto: OUP The Oxford Trollope, 2 vols, intro to political novels Michael Sadleir, preface Sir Edward Marsh, ill Lynton Lamb; reprinted 1973; paperback 1973.
1972　L: Penguin Books, intro & notes Stephen Wall; reprinted 1974, 1978.

1973　L: Panther Books, intro Simon Raven.
1982　L/OUP World's Classics, foreword W.J. McCormack, preface Norman St John Stevas, intro Kate Flint, ed Andrew Swarbrick, ill Lynton Lamb.
1989　L: Trollope Society, intro David Skilton.
　　　L: Folio Society, as above, ill L. Thomas.

23. MISS MACKENZIE

Written: 22 May - 18 August 1864.
MS: New York Public Library, New York (Berg Collection).
Book publication:
1865　L: Chapman & Hall, 2 vols; in 1 vol 1866; Select Library of Fiction no 122 1868, 1871, 5th edn, 4th edn 1872, 1879.
　　　NY: Harper, Library of Select Novels no 253.
1871　L/NY: Routledge.
1876　Berlin: Engelmann, Asher's Library, 2 vols.
　　　Arnhem: Rinkes, 2 vols (Dutch - **Miss Mackenzie**, trans J. Ebbeler).
1880　L: Ward Lock, Select Library of Fiction no 8.
1881　NY: Munro, Seaside Library.
1924　L: OUP World's Classics no 278; reprinted 1936, 1950.
1981　NY: Arno Press, 2 vols, intro Juliet McMaster.
1987　N.Y: Dover Publications.
1988　L: OUP World's Classics, ed A.O.J. Cockshut.

24. HUNTING SKETCHES

Serialised: Pall Mall Gazette, Feb-Mar 1865.
Book publication:
1865　L: Chapman & Hall; 1866 (twice).
1929　Hartford, Conn: Mitchell, ill Ned King, intro C. Ellsworth Smith.
1933　NY: Gosden Head / L: Hutchinson [1934], ill Robert Ball, intro James Boyd.
1952　L: Benn / USA: John Day [1953], ill and intro Lionel Edwards.
1967　NY: Arno Press, Abercrombie & Fitch Library.
1981　NY: Arno Press, intro Nina Burgis.

23. THE BELTON ESTATE

Written: 30 January - 4 September 1865.
MS: Huntington Library, San Marino, California.
Serialised: Fortnightly Review, 15 May 1865-1 Jan 1866, vols 1-3. Littell's Living Age, Jul 1865- Jan 1866, vol 88. Revue Nationale, Jan-Jul 1867 (French - **L'Heritage des Belton**).

Book publication:
1866   L: Chapman & Hall, 3 vols; reprinted twice
        same year; in 1 vol 1866; Select Library of
        Fiction no 125 1868 (3rd edn).
        Philadelphia: Lippincott 1871 (7th edn).
        NY: Harper, Library of Select Novels no
        263.
        Leipzig: Tauchnitz, 2 vols.
1867   Dordrecht, Netherlands: Brast, 2 vols (Dutch
        - **Het Huis Belton**, trans M.P. Lindo).
1871   L/NY: Routledge.
        St Petersburg: (Russian - **Beltonskoy
        Pomesti**).
1875   Paris: Hachette (French - **La Domaine de
        Belton**, trans E. Daillac); reprinted 1875,
        1882.
1880   L: Ward Lock, Select Library of Fiction no
9;   further issue 1894.
1882   NY: Munro, Seaside Library.
1912   NY: Dodd, Mead, 2 vols.
1923   L: OUP World's Classics no 251; reprinted
        1930, 1951, 1958, 1964, 1969.
1985   NY: Dover Publications.
1985   L: OUP World's Classics, ed John Halperin.
1991   L: Trollope Society, intro David Skilton.
        L: Folio Society, as above, ill A. Rendle.

26. TRAVELLING SKETCHES

Serialised: Pall Mall Gazette, Aug-Sep 1865.
Book publication:
1866   L: Chapman & Hall.
1981   NY: Arno Press, intro Asa Briggs.

27. CLERGYMEN OF THE CHURCH OF ENGLAND

Serialised: Pall Mall Gazette, Nov 1865 - Jan 1866.
Book publication:
1866   L: Chapman & Hall.
1974   Leicester, England: Leicester University
        Press, intro Ruth apRoberts.

28. NINA BALATKA

Written: 11 September - 31 December 1865.
MS: New York Public Library, New York (Arents
Collection).
Serialised: Blackwood's Magazine, Jul 1866-Jan
1867, vols 100-101; Littell's Living Age, 13 Oct 1866
- 9 Feb 1867, vols 91-92.
Book publication:
1867   Edinburgh: Blackwood, 2 vols; reissue in one
        vol 1879, with attribution to A.T. (previously
        published anonymously).
        Leipzig: Tauchnitz.
        Boston: Littell & Gay.

1946   L/NY: OUP World's Classics no 505 (with
        Linda Tressel).
[1959?] Peking: Chinese translation.
1981   NY: Arno Press, 2 vols, intro James Gindin.
1991   L: OUP World's Classics, ed Robert Tracy
        (with **Linda Tressel**).

29. THE LAST CHRONICLE OF BARSET

Written: 20 January - 5 September 1866.
MS: Yale University, New Haven, Connecticut
(Beinecke Library).
Part issue: 32 weekly parts 1 Dec 1866-8 Jul 1867
(L: Smith, Elder).
Book publication:
1867   NY: Harper.
        L: Smith, Elder, 2 vols, ill George H.
        Thomas, new edn. 2 vols 1876; Illustrated
        Edition of Popular Works 1869; in 1 vol
        1872, 1876.
        Leipzig: Tauchnitz, 3 vols.
1869   Arnhem: Thiems, 3 vols (Dutch - **De
        Verluten Wissel**).
1879   L: Chapman & Hall, 2 vols, vols 7-8 of **The
        Chronicles of Barsetshire**, fp F.A. Fraser;
        further issues 1885, 1889, 1893.
1883   NY: Munro, Seaside Library, 2 parts.
1892   NY: Dodd, Mead, 3 vols; further issues
1903,   1929.
1900   Philadelphia: Gebbie, 3 vols; Collector's
        Edition vols 11-13.
1906   L: Bell / NY: Macmillan [1907], 2 vols;
        reprinted 1926; in 1 vol 1910, 1923, 1928;
        Bohn's Popular Library 1914.
1909   L: Dent / NY: Dutton, Everyman's Library, 2
        vols, nos.391-392, intro Ernest Rhys;
        reprinted 1912, 1922, 1928, 1936, 1966,
        1979.
        L: Routledge / NY: Dutton, ill George H.
        Thomas.
1914   L: Nelson, New Century Library; Nelson's
        Classics, 2 vols, 1926; in 1 vol 1934, 1954.
1924   L: Bell / NY: Harcourt [1925], 2 vols.
1925   L: Hayes, ill George H. Thomas.
1926   Boston: Lauriat.
[1927?] L: Waverley, ill George H. Thomas.
1928   L: Lane, 2 vols.
1929   Oxford: Blackwell, Shakespeare Head
        Press, 4 vols.
1932   L/NY: OUP World's Classics, 2 vols, nos
        198-199; in 1 vol 1946, 1948, 1951; intro
        Bradford A. Booth 1958, 1961.
1945   Stockholm: Modern Varldslitteratur, 2 vols
        (Swedish - **Barsets Sista Kronika**, trans
        Margareta Angstrom).
1949   L: Chatto & Windus, Zodiac Press; reprinted
        1961, 1973 / NY: Grove Press, 1952.
1952   Oslo: Mortensens, 2 vols (Norwegian -
        Farvel til Barset).

1957 L: OUP Sheldon Library, abridged Griselda
Taylor, ill Philip Gough.
1961 Toronto: Macleod, intro Gerald Warner
Brace.
1964 Cambridge, Mass.: Riverside Press, intro A.
Mizener; reprinted paperback 1989.
NY: Norton, intro Gerald Warner Brace.
1967 L: Pan Books, intro Walter Allen, notes
Arthur Calder-Marshall.
L: Penguin Books, intro Laurence Lerner, ed
Peter Fairclough.
1969 L: Heritage Press, 2 vols, intro Courtland
Canby, ill Jemima Ede.
1980 L: Folio Society, intro Julian Symons, ill
Peter Reddick.
L: OUP World's Classics, intro Stephen Gill.
1989 NY: OUP

30. THE CLAVERINGS

Written: 24 August 1863 - 31 July 1864.
MS: Princeton University, Princeton, New Jersey
(Taylor Collection).
Serialised: Cornhill, Feb 1866-May 1867, vols 13-15;
Galaxy, May 1866-Mar 1867, vols 1-3; Littell's
Living Age, 1866-1867, vols 88-92. Also issued in
parts 1866-1867 (NY: Church).
Book publication:
1866 NY: Harper, ill., Library of Select Novels no
286 (issued 1867).
1867 NY: Church.
L: Smith, Elder, 2 vols, ill M. Ellen Edwards;
in 1 vol Illustrated Editions of Popular
Works 1871; further issues 1872, 1881.
Leipzig: Tauchnitz, 2 vols.
Dordrecht, Netherlands: Brast, 2 vols (Dutch
- **De Claverings**, trans J.C. Deventer).
St Petersburg: 2 vols (Russian - **Klaveringi**).
1871 Boston: Littell & Gay.
1875 Stavanger: A. Moe, 2 vols (Norwegian -
Familien Clavering).
1910 L: Collins.
1924 L: OUP World's Classics no 252, intro G.S.
Street; reprinted 1929, 1957, 1959, 1979.
1977 NY: Dover Publications, ill M. Ellen
Edwards, intro Norman Donaldson. Restores
part of chapter 6 missing from previous book
editions.
1986 L: OUP World's Classics, ed David Skilton.

31. LOTTA SCHMIDT AND OTHER STORIES

Comprising *Lotta Schmidt, The Adventures of Fred
Pickering, The Two Generals, Father Giles of
Ballymoy, Malachi's Cove, The Widow's Mite, The
Last American who left Venice, Miss Ophelia Gledd,
The Journey to Panama.*
Book Publication:

1867 L: Strahan; further edns 1867, 1870.
1870 L: Chapman & Hall; Select Library of
Fiction no 188 1871.
1871 L/NY: Routledge.
1874 Berlin: Engelmann, Asher's Library, as
Fred Pickering and Other Stories.
1880 L: Ward Lock, Select Library of Fiction
no 10; further issue 1882.
1981 NY: Arno Press, intro Reginald Terry.

32. PROSPECTUS FOR SAINT PAUL'S MAGAZINE

1867 L: Virtue. A 4pp prospectus for the magazine
begun under A.T.'s editorship in 1867. See
item A111.

33. LINDA TRESSEL

Written: 2 June - 16 July 1867.
Serialised: Blackwood's Magazine, Oct 1867-May
1868, vols 102-3; Littell's Living Age, 1867-8, vols
95-7.
Book publication:
1868 Edinburgh: Blackwood, 2 vols; reissue in one
vol 1879, with attribution to A.T. (previously
published anonymously).
Boston: Littell & Gay.
1946 L/NY: OUP World's Classics no 505, with
Nina Balatka.
1981 NY: Arno Press, 2 vols, intro James Gindin.
1991 L: OUP World's Classics, ed Robert Tracy
(with **Nina Balatka**).

34. BRITISH SPORTS AND PASTIMES

Articles from *Saint Paul's Magazine:* ed and with a
preface by A.T., and including his essay 'On Hunting'
(originally pbd as 'About Hunting' in *Saint Paul's*).
Book publication:
1868 L: Virtue & Co. / NY: Virtue & Yorston;
further issues under imprints Virtue,
Spalding & Co., Strahan & Co., Daldy,
Isbister & Co.

35. PHINEAS FINN

Written: 17 November 1866 - 15 May 1867.
MS: Yale University, New Haven, Connecticut
(Beinecke Library).
Serialised: Saint Paul's Magazine, Oct 1867 - May
1869, vols 1-4; Littell's Living Age, 1867-69, vols 95-
101; New Eclectic, 1867-69, vols 1-4.
Book publication:
1868 NY: Harper.
1869 L: Virtue, 2 vols, ill Millais; reissued 1871

L: Chapman & Hall, Select Library of Modern Fiction no 186.
Leipzig: Tauchnitz, 3 vols.

1870   L: Strahan.
Arnhem: Nijhoff, 3 vols (Dutch - **Phineas Finn**, trans J.H. Maronier).

1871   L/NY: Routledge.

1873   St Petersburg: 2 vols (Russian - **Phineas Finn, Irlandskijy Chlen Parlamenta**).

1880   L: Ward Lock, Select Library of Fiction no 24.

1882   NY: Munro, Seaside Library, 2 parts.

1893   NY: Dodd, Mead, 3 vols.

1901   Philadelphia: Gebbie, 3 vols, Collector's Edition vols 17-19.

1911   L: Bell / NY: Macmillan, 2 vols, intro Frederic Harrison.

1929   L: Dent / NY: Dutton, Everyman's Library, 2 vols, nos.832-833, intro Hugh Walpole.

1937   L/NY: OUP World's Classics, 2 vols, nos 447,448; reprinted 1944; in 1 vol 1951, 1957, 1962.

1949   L/NY/Toronto: OUP The Oxford Trollope, 2 vols, intro Sir Shane Leslie, ill T.L.B. Huskinson, notes R.W. Chapman; reprinted 1973; paperback 1973.

1968   L: Panther Books, intro Herbert van Thal; intro Simon Raven 1973.

1972   L: Penguin Books, intro & notes John Sutherland.

1977   NY: Berkeley, Medallion Books, intro Simon Raven.

1982   L: OUP World's Classics, foreword W.J. McCormack, ed and intro Jacques Berthoud, ill T.L.B. Huskinson.

1989   L: Trollope Society, intro J. Enoch Powell.
L: Folio Society, as above, ill L. Thomas.

1991   N.Y: OUP ed Jacques Berthoud.

36. HE KNEW HE WAS RIGHT

Written: 13 November 1867 - 12 June 1868.
MS: Pierpont Morgan Library, New York.
Part issue: 32 weekly (also 8 monthly) parts, 17 Oct 1868 - 22 May 1869 (L: Virtue).
Serialised: Every Saturday, Oct 1868 - May 1869, vols 6-7; Eclectic Magazine, 1868-1869, vols 71 3.
Book publication:
1869   L: Strahan, 2 vols, ill Marcus Stone; in 1 vol 1870.
NY: Harper, 2 vols; in 1 vol 1870.
Leipzig: Tauchnitz, 3 vols.

1870   Schiedam, Netherlands: Roelants, 3 vols (Dutch - **Wie Heefts Gelijl ?**, trans J.C. Van Deventer).
St Petersburg: 3 vols (Russian - **On Anal On Bil Prav**), further issue 1873.

1871   L: Chapman & Hall, Select Library of Fiction no 187, 1878.

L/NY: Routledge.

1880   L: Ward Lock, Select Library of Fiction no 25.

1948   L/NY: OUP World's Classics no 507; reprinted 1951, 1963, 1978.

1974   Brisbane: University of Queensland Press, ed P.D. Edwards / L: Batsford, 1981.

1983   NY: Dover Publications.

1985   L: OUP World's Classics, ed John Sutherland.

37. DID HE STEAL IT?

Three act play by A.T. adapted from **The Last Chronicle of Barset**.
Written: February/March 1869. Not performed.
Book publication:
1869   L: Virtue & Co., privately printed.

1952   Princeton: Princeton University Library, intro Robert H. Taylor, limited to 1000 copies.

1981   NY: Arno Press, with **The Noble Jilt**, foreword Robert H. Taylor.

38. ON ENGLISH PROSE FICTION AS A RATIONAL AMUSEMENT

Written: late 1869
Book publication:
[1869?]   Privately printed for A.T., 44pp pamphlet.

1938   L: Constable, ed and intro Morris L. Parrish, limited to 150 copies. With three other lectures (items A19, A20 and A42).

1976   Philadelphia: Folcroft.

39. THE VICAR OF BULLHAMPTON

Written: 15 June - November 1868.
MS: Harvard University, Cambridge, Massachusetts (Houghton Library).
Part issue: 11 monthly parts, Jul 1869 - May 1870 (L: Bradbury & Evans).
Serialised: Lippincott's Magazine, 1869-70, vols 4-5.
Book publication:
1869-70 Philadelphia: Lippincott, 2 vols; in 1 vol 1870.

1870   L: Bradbury & Evans, ill H. Woods; further issue 1871.
NY: Harper.
Leipzig: Tauchnitz, 2 vols.
Moscow: (Russian - **Bullhamptonsky Vikaryi**).

1872   Schiedam, Netherlands: Roelants, 2 vols (Dutch - **De Predikant van Bullhampton**, trans Mw van Deventer).

1873   St Petersburg: 2 vols (Russian - **Bullhamptonsky Vikaryi**).

1875	L: Chapman & Hall, Select Library of Fiction no 300.
1880	L: Ward Lock, Select Library of Fiction no 15.
1883	NY: Munro, Seaside Library.
1906	NY: Dodd, Mead, 2 vols.
1924	L: OUP World's Classics no 272, reprinted 1933, 1950, 1963, 1978.
1979	NY: Dover Publications.
1983	Gloucester, England: Alan Sutton, intro Nicholas Mander.
1988	L: OUP World's Classics, ed David Skilton.

40. AN EDITOR'S TALES

Comprising *The Turkish Bath, Mary Gresley, Josephine de Montmorenci, The Panjandrum, The Spotted Dog, Mrs Brumby.*
Book publication:

1870	L: Strahan.
1871	L: Chapman & Hall, entitled **Mary Gresley and An Editor's Tales**; Select Library of Fiction no 192 1871, 1873; under original title 1873. L/NY: Routledge, entitled **Mary Gresley, or, An Editor's Tales**.
1880	L: Ward Lock, Select Library of Fiction no 11; 1883 6th edn.
1981	NY: Arno Press, intro Donald D. Stone.

41. THE COMMENTARIES OF CAESAR

Written: 29 January - 25 April 1870.
Book publication:

1870	Edinburgh: Blackwood, Ancient Classics for English Readers; reissued in 1873 with Tacitus by W.B. Donne (undated new general title) reprinted 1887, 1897, 1899.
1872	Philadelphia: Lippincott, Ancient Classics for English Readers.
1981	NY: Arno Press, intro Ruth apRoberts.

42. HIGHER EDUCATION OF WOMEN

Written: ?1868-70
Book publication:
[1869-70?] Privately printed for A.T., 32pp pamphlet.

1938	L: Constable, ed and intro Morris L. Parrish, limited to 150 copies. With three other lectures (items A19, A20 and A38).
1976	Philadelphia: Folcroft.

43. SIR HARRY HOTSPUR OF HUMBLETHWAITE

Written: December 1868 - 30 January 1869.
MS: Yale University, New Haven, Connecticut (Beinecke Library)
Serialised: Macmillan's Magazine, May-Dec 1870, vols 22-23; Lippincott's Magazine 1870, vols 5-6.
Book publication:

1871	L: Hurst & Blackett [issued 1870]. L/NY: Macmillan. NY: Harper, Library of Select Novels no 354. Leipzig: Tauchnitz. Amsterdam: Leendertz (Dutch - **Emily Hotspur of hoe een Maisje Kan Leifhebben**, trans S.J. Andriessen). St Petersburg (Russian - **Sir Harry Hotspur**).
1879	L: Chapman & Hall, Select Library of Fiction no 365. NY: Munro, Seaside Library.
1880	L: Ward Lock, Select Library of Fiction no 16.
1928	L/NY: OUP World's Classics no 336.
1948	L: Williams & Norgate.
1981	NY: Arno Press, intro John Halperin.
1986	NY: Dover Publications.

44. RALPH THE HEIR

Written: 4 April - 7 August 1869.
MS: Harvard University, Cambridge, Massachusetts (Houghton Library).
Part issue: 19 monthly parts, Jan 1870 - Jul 1871 (L: Strahan).
Serialised: Saint Paul's Magazine, Supplement, Jan 1870 - Jul 1871, vols 5-8; Appleton's Journal, Supplement, Feb 1870 - May 1871, vols 3-5.
Book publication:

1871	NY: Harper. L: Hurst & Blackett, 3 vols. Leipzig: Tauchnitz, 2 vols. L: Strahan; reissued 1872 L/NY: Routledge, with new title page. St Petersburg: 2 vols (Russian - **Naslednik Ralph**).
1872	L: Chapman & Hall, Select Library of Fiction no 203; further issue 1874. Denmark: Jordan, 2 vols (Danish - **Arvingden Ralph**).
1874	Stockholm: Flodin (Swedish - **Ralph**).
1880	L: Ward Lock, Select Library of Fiction no 12.
1886	NY: Munro, Seaside Library.
1939	L/NY: OUP World's Classics, 2 vols, nos. 475-476; in 1 vol 1951.
1978	NY: Dover Publications.
1990	L: OUP World's Classics, ed John Sutherland.

45. THE GOLDEN LION OF GRANPERE

Written: 1 September - 22 October 1867.
Serialised: Good Words, Jan-Aug 1872; Harper's Magazine, Feb-Sep 1872, vols 44-45.
Book publication:
1872   L: Tinsley; further issue 1873; ill F.A. Fraser 1873.
      NY: Harper.
      Leipzig: Tauchnitz.
      Amsterdam: Kampen (Dutch - **Het Hotel de Gouden Leeuw**, trans Mw v. Westerheene).
1873   St Petersburg (Russian - **Zolotoy Lyev v Granpere**).
      Leipzig: Schlide (German - **Der Goldene Lowe in Granpere**, trans Lina Kayser).
1875   L: Routledge, Railway Library no 666.
1885   L: Chatto & Windus.
      NY: Munro, Seaside Library.
1924   L: Dent / NY: Dutton, Everyman's Library no 761, intro Hugh Walpole.
1946   L/NY: OUP World's Classics no 504.
1981   NY: Arno Press, intro David Skilton.

46. THE EUSTACE DIAMONDS

Written: 4 December 1869 - 25 August 1870.
MS: Princeton University Library, Princeton, New Jersey (Taylor Collection).
Serialised: Fortnightly Review, 1 Jul 1871-1 Feb 1873, vols 16-19; Galaxy, Sep 1871-Jan 1873, vols 12-15.
Book publication:
1872   NY: Harper; further issue 1873.
1873   L: Chapman & Hall, 3 vols; in 1 vol, Select Library of Fiction no 243 1874.
      Berlin: Engelmann, Asher's Library, 2 vols.
      St Petersburg: 2 vols (Russian - **Brillyanstovoy Ojyrly / Brillyanti Ustasov**).
1873   Groningen: Erven Bv. d. Kemp, 3 vols (Dutch - **De Diamanten der Familie Eustace**, trans J.W. Straatman).
      Amsterdam: Syrbrandi (Dutch - **De Zorgen van een Rijk Weeuwtje**).
      L/NY: Routledge.
1881   L: Ward Lock, Select Library of Fiction no 26.
1902   Philadelphia: Gebbie, 2 vols, Collector's Edition vols 20/21.
1903   NY: Dodd, Mead, 2 vols.
1930   L/NY: OUP World's Classics no 357; reprinted 1941, 1942, 1952, 1953, 1960; intro Michael Sadleir 1968.
1947   NY: Modern Library.
1950   L/NY/Toronto: OUP The Oxford Trollope, 2 vols, intro Michael Sadleir, ill Blair Hughes-Stanton; reprinted in 1 vol and as paperback 1973.

1951   NY: Garden City Publishing Co., ill Kenneth Riley, abridged.
1968   L: Panther Books, intro Herbert van Thal; intro Simon Raven 1973.
1969   L: Penguin Books, ed and intro Stephen Gill & John Sutherland.
1977   NY: Berkeley Medallion Books, intro Simon Raven.
1983   L: OUP World's Classics, ed and intro W.J. McCormack, ill Blair Hughes-Stanton.
1990   L: Trollope Society, intro P.D.James.
      L: Folio Society, as above, ill L. Thomas.
1991   N.Y: OUP ed W.J. McCormack.

47. AUSTRALIA AND NEW ZEALAND

Written: 23 October 1871 - 15 December 1872.
MS: National Library of Australia, Canberra.
Serialised: Australasian, 22 Feb 1873 - 20 Jun 1874.
Book publication:
1873   L: Chapman & Hall, 2 vols; reprinted 1875, 1876; as 4 separate books, **New Zealand**, **Victoria & Tasmania**, **New South Wales & Queensland** and **South Australia & Western Australia**, 1874, 1875.
      Melbourne: Robertson, 6 vols, 1873; also 1 vol. 1873, 1874. Leipzig: Tauchnitz, 3 vols.
1875   Leiden: Noothoven Van Goor, 2 vols (Dutch - **Reis Door Australia en Nieuw-Zeeland**).
1884   L: Ward Lock, as 4 separate books.
1947   Wellington, N.Z.: A.H. & A.W. Reed, **The Story of Otago** (by A.H. Reed) containing chapters 3-4 of **New Zealand** pp 333-67, ill.
1966   Melbourne: Nelson, abridged and ed Hume Dow, entitled **Trollope's Australia**, ill.
1967   St Lucia, Queensland: University of Queensland Press, ed D.P. Edwards & R.B. Joyce, entitled **Australia**, omitting chapters on New Zealand.
1968   L: Dawson, 2 vols.
1987   Gloucester, England: Alan Sutton, 2 vols. Paperback, omitting chapters on New Zealand.

48. LADY ANNA

Written: 25 May - 19 July 1871.
MS: Princeton University, Princeton, New Jersey (Taylor Collection).
Serialised: Fortnightly Review, Apr 1873-Apr 1874, vols 19-21; Australasian, 1873-1874; Vestnik Evropy, nos.5-9, 11-12 (1873) and 1-4 (1874) - Russian translation.
Book publication:
1873   Leipzig: Tauchnitz, 2 vols.
      NY: Harper, Library of Select Novels no 411.
      L: Chapman & Hall, 2 vols; in 1 vol same

year; Select Library of Fiction no 244 1875;
new edn 1879.

Moscow (Russian - **Lady Anna**).

	Toronto: Hunter Rose.
1878	Detroit: Craig & Taylor.
1880	L: Ward Lock, Select Library of Fiction no 14.
1882	NY: Munro, Seaside Library.
1936	L/NY: OUP World's Classics no 443; reprinted 1950.
1942	L: Classics Book Club.
1981	NY: Arno Press, 2 vols, intro J.Hillis Miller.
1984	NY: Dover Publications.
1986	Gloucester, England: Alan Sutton.
1990	L: Trollope Society, intro Paul Johnson.
	L: Folio Society, as above, ill B. Wilkinson.
	L: OUP World's Classics, ed Stephen Orgel.

49. PHINEAS REDUX

Written: 23 October 1870 - 1 April 1871.
MS: Yale University, New Haven, Connecticut
(Beinecke Library).
Serialised: Graphic, 19 Jul 1873-10 Jan 1874, vols 8-9.
Book publication:

1874	L: Chapman & Hall, 2 vols, ill Frank Holl, also reissue by Chapman & Hall 2 vols in 1; in 1 vol Select Library of Fiction no 267 1875, 1876, 1878 4th edn.
	NY: Harper.
	Berlin: Engelmann, Asher's Library, 3 vols.
	L/NY: Routledge.
	St Petersburg: 2 vols (Russian - **Phineas Finn, Vozrativmyisya Nazad**).
1881	L: Ward Lock, Select Library of Fiction no 27.
1883	NY: Munro, Seaside Library, 2 parts.
1893	NY: Dodd, Mead, 3 vols.
1902	Philadelphia: Gebbie, 3 vols, Collector's Edition vols 22-4.
1911	L: Bell / NY: Macmillan, 2 vols; further issue 1913.
1937	L/NY: OUP World's Classics, 2 vols, nos. 450-1; in 1 vol 1952, 1957, 1964; intro R.W. Chapman 1970.
1951	L/NY/Toronto: OUP The Oxford Trollope, 2 vols, intro R.W. Chapman, ill T.L.B. Huskinson; in 1 vol 1973; paperback 1973.
1973	L: Panther Books, intro Simon Raven NY: Berkeley Medallion Books 1977.
1983	L: OUP World's Classics, intro F.S.L. Lyons, ed John C. Wale, ill T.L.B. Huskinson.
1991	N.Y: OUP ed John C. Wale.

50. HARRY HEATHCOTE OF GANGOIL

Written: 1-28 January 1873.
MS: Yale University, New Haven, Connecticut
(Beinecke Library).
Serialised: Graphic, Christmas Number 1873, vol 8;
Littell's Living Age, 24 Jan - 7 Mar 1874, vol 120.
Book publication:

1874	NY: Harper, Library of Select Novels no 407.
	Leipzig: Tauchnitz.
	L: Sampson Low; further issue same year, 1875; ill edn 1874.
1875	St Petersburg: (Russian - **Henrik Heathcote in Gangoily**).
1883	L: Ward Lock, Select Library of Fiction no 21.
1885	NY: Munro Seaside Library, pocket edn. Glasgow: Grand Colosseum Warehouse Co. (3rd Edn).
1963	L/Melbourne: Angus & Robertson, intro Marcie Muir, ill
1981	NY: Arno Press, intro P.D. Edwards.
1986	Gloucester, England: Alan Sutton.
1987	NY: Dover Publications.

51. THE WAY WE LIVE NOW

Written: 1 May - 2 December 1873.
MS: Pierpont Morgan Library, New York.
Part issue: 20 monthly parts, Feb 1874 - Sep 1875 (L: Chapman & Hall).
Serialised: Old & New, Jan 1874 - May 1875, vols 9-11 (omitting chapters 77-100).
Book publication:

1875	L: Chapman & Hall, 2 vols, ill Lionel Faulkes, reissued 2 vols in 1 1875.
	NY: Harper.
	Leipzig: Tauchnitz, 4 vols.
1876	L: Chatto & Windus, 2 vols; in 1 vol 1879, 1907.
1877	St Petersburg: 4 vols (Russian - **Kak my teper' Zhiviam**).
1883	NY: Munro, Seaside Library, 2 parts.
1941	L/NY: OUP World's Classics, 2 vols, nos. 48-5; and in 1 vol; reprinted 1951, 1957, 1962, 1968.
1950	NY: Knopf, intro Marion E. Dodd.
1969	L: Panther Books, intro Herbert van Thal.
1974	Indianapolis: Bobbs Merrill, intro Robert Tracy.
1982	L: OUP World's Classics, intro and notes John Sutherland.
	NY: Dover Publications.

52. THE PRIME MINISTER

Written: 2 April - 15 September 1874.
MS: New York Public Library, New York (Arents Collection).
Part issue: 8 monthly parts, Nov 1875-Jun 1876 (L: Chapman & Hall).
Book publication:
1876   NY: Harper.
        L: Chapman & Hall, 4 vols; in 1 vol 1876, 1877; Select Library of Fiction no 362 1877, 1878.
        Leipzig: Tauchnitz, 4 vols.
        Toronto: Bedford Brothers.
1877   Philadelphia: Porter & Coates.
        St Petersburg: (Russian - **Premer Ministr**).
        NY: Lovell, Oxford Edn.
        NY: National Book Co.
1881   L: Ward Lock, Select Library of Fiction no 28.
1886   NY: Munro, Seaside Library, 2 parts.
1893   NY: Dodd, Mead, 3 vols.
1902   Philadelphia: Gebbie, 3 vols, Collector's Edn vols 25-7.
1938   L/NY: OUP World's Classics, 2 vols, nos. 454-5, and 1 vol; reprinted 1951, 1955, 1961, 1968.
1952   L/NY/Toronto: OUP The Oxford Trollope, 2 vols, intro L.S. Amery, ill Hecktor Whistler; reprinted 1973; paperback 1973.
1973   L: Panther Books, intro Simon Raven / NY: Berkeley Medallion Books 1977.
1984   L: OUP World's Classics, intro John McCormack, ed Jennifer Uglow.
1991   N.Y: OUP ed Jennifer Uglow
        L: Trollope Society, intro Asa Briggs.
        L: Folio Society, as above, ill L. Thomas.

53. THE AMERICAN SENATOR

Written: 4 June - 24 September 1875.
MS: Princeton University, Princeton, New Jersey (Taylor Collection).
Serialised: Temple Bar, May 1876-Jul 1877, vols 47-50.
Book publication:
1877   L: Chapman & Hall, 3 vols.
        NY: Harper, Library of Select Novels.
        NY: Munro, Seaside Library.
        Toronto: Bedford Brothers.
        Detroit: Craig & Taylor.
        Leipzig: Tauchnitz, 3 vols.
        Copenhagen: Berlin Tid, 2 vols (Danish - **En Vinter i Dillsborough**).
1878   L: Chatto & Windus; further issues 1879, 1886.
1931   L/NY: OUP World's Classics no 391; reprinted 1951, 1962.
1940   NY: Random House, preface A. Edward

Newton, intro Henry S. Drinker.
1979   NY: Dover Publication.
1981   NY: Arno Press, intro Robert H. Taylor.
1986   L: OUP World's Classics, ed John Halperin.

54. CHRISTMAS AT THOMPSON HALL

Written: 1876.
Magazine publication: Graphic Christmas Number 1876.
Book publication:
1877   NY: Harper, Harper's Half Hour Series, with fp.
1885   L: Sampson Low, entitled **Thompson Hall**, ill W.R.
1891   Einsideln, Switzerland: Benziger, Familien-bibliothek, Ausgewählte erzehtungen und schilderungen, V ser, no 19, pp [35]-56 (German - **Das Weinachtsfest zu Thompsonhall**), ill Alice Salzbraun.
1894   Boston: J. Knight, Cosy Corner Series, with fp.
1901   Boston: L.C. Page, Day's Work Series.
1912   Berlin: Scherl (English/German - **Weinachten in Thompson Hall**).
1979   Racine, Wisconsin: Caledonia Press, preface John Kingsley Shannon.

55. SOUTH AFRICA

Written: 23 July 1877 - 2 January 1878.
MS: Huntington Library, San Marino, California.
Book publication:
1878   L: Chapman & Hall, 2 vols; three further editions same year; in 1 vol (abridged and with new matter in preface and chapter XI) 1879.
        Leipzig: Tauchnitz, 2 vols.
1939   L: Longman, abridged, intro and notes P. Haworth.
1968   L: Dawson, 2 vols.
1973   Cape Town: A.A. Balkema, intro and notes J.H. Davidson.
1987   Gloucester, England: Alan Sutton, 2 vol. paperback.

56. IS HE POPENJOY?

Written: 12 October 1874 - 3 May 1875.
Serialised: All the Year Round, 13 Oct 1877 - 13 Jul 1878, vols 39-41.
Book publication:
1878   L: Chapman & Hall, 3 vols; in 1 vol same year, 1879 3rd edn; Select Library of Fiction no 384 1879.
        NY: Harper, Franklin Square Library no 1.
        Leipzig: Tauchnitz, 3 vols.

St Petersburg: (Russian - **Popenjoy li on?**).
Strasbourg: Schultz, 3 vols (German - **Ist er Popenjoy?**).
1880   L: Ward Lock, Select Library of Fiction no 17; further issue [1882], 1883.
1883   NY: Munro, Seaside Library.
1907   NY: Dodd, Mead, 2 vols, fp Walter H. Everett; further issue 1913.
1944   L/NY: OUP World's Classics, 2 vols, nos. 492, 493; also 1 vol; reprinted 1 vol 1946, 1948, 1951, 1965.
1986   L: OUP World's Classics, ed John Sutherland.

57. ICELAND

Magazine publication: Fortnightly Review, 1 Aug 1878, 30:175-90.
Book publication:
1878   L: privately printed, 28pp pamphlet.

58. HOW THE 'MASTIFFS' WENT TO ICELAND

Written: August 1878.
Book publication:
1878   L: Virtue & Co.; ill Mrs Hugh Blackburn. Not published. (Note: Mrs Blackburn's account of the same voyage was serialised in Good Words, 1879, Jun:429-32, Jul:480-6, Aug: 559-65, Sep:622-8, with five of the same and ten other illustrations.)
1971   Reykjavik: Icelandic translation.
1981   NY: Arno Press, intro Coral Lansbury.

59. THE LADY OF LAUNAY

MS: Huntington Library, San Marino, California.
Serialised: Light, 6 April - 11 May 1878.
Book publication:
1878   NY: Harper, Harper's Half Hour Series. NY: Munro, Seaside Library, with **Lilian's Husband**, by Annie A. Gibbs.
1978   Racine, Wisconsin: Caledonia Press.

60. AN EYE FOR AN EYE

Written: 13 September - 10 October 1870.
MS: Princeton University, Princeton, New Jersey (Parrish Collection).
Serialised: Whitehall Review, 24 Aug 1878 - 1 Feb 1879.
Book publication:
1879   L: Chapman & Hall, 2 vols; in 1 vol St James's Library & Select Library of Fiction no 404 same year.

NY: Harper, Franklin Square Library no 37.
Leipzig: Tauchnitz.
Neuchâtel: Sandoz et Fischbacher (French - **Oeil pour Oeil**, trans Amy Davy).
1880   NY: Munro, Seaside Library.
1881   St Petersburg (Russian - **Oko za Oko**).
L: Ward Lock, Select Library of Fiction no 18.
1887   Budapest (Hungarian - **Szemet - Szemet**).
1946   Brussels Editions La Boetie (French - **Oeil pour Oeil**).
1955   Antwerp (Flemish translation).
1966   L: Anthony Blond / NY: Stein & Day, Doughty Library, intro Simon Raven.
1979   NY: Garland, 2 vols, intro Robert Lee Wolff.
1981   NY: Arno Press, 2 vols, intro James R. Kincaid.

61. THACKERAY

Written: 1 February - 25 March 1879.
Book publication:
1879   L: Macmillan, English Men of Letters Series; reprinted 1880, 1882, 1886, 1887, 1892, 1895, 1900, 1905, 1906, 1909, 1912, 1925.
NY: Harper, English Men of Letters Series; Franklin Square Library no 144 1880; Handy Series 1887; Portrait Edn 1894, 1899, 1902. Toronto: James Dykes Campbell.
1880   Leipzig: Martigs Berl (German - **William M. Thackeray**, trans and with comments by L. Katscher).
1894   NY: Lovell.
1906   NY: Macmillan; reprinted 1909.
1968   Detroit: Gale Research Co.

62. JOHN CALDIGATE

Written: 3 February - 22 July 1877
MS: New York Public Library, New York (Arents Collection).
Serialised: Blackwood's Magazine, Apr 1878 - Jun 1879, vols 123-125.
Book publication:
1879   L: Chapman & Hall, 3 vols; bound as 1 vol same year.
NY: Harper, Franklin Square Library no 63.
NY: Munro, Seaside Library.
Leipzig: Tauchnitz, 3 vols.
1880   L: Routledge, Railway Library.
1885   L: Chatto & Windus; further issues 1909, 1922.
1907   NY: Dodd, Mead, 2 vols, fp Walter H. Everett; further issue 1911.
1946   L/NY: OUP World's Classics no 502; reprinted 1952, 1961.
1972   L: Chatto & Windus, Zodiac Press.

63. COUSIN HENRY

Written: 26 October - 8 December 1878.
MS: Yale University, New Haven, Connecticut (Beinecke Library).
Serialised: Simultaneously in Manchester Weekly Times and North British Weekly, 8 Mar - 24 May 1879.
Book publication:
1879   NY: Munro, Seaside Library.
        L: Chapman & Hall, 2 vols; in 1 vol Select Library of Fiction no 408 1880; Select Authors 1881.
        NY: Harper, Franklin Square Library no 83.
        Leipzig: Tauchnitz.
1881   L: Ward Lock, Select Library of Fiction no 19.
        Paris: Hachette (French - **Le Cousin Henry**, trans Mme Honorine Martel).
1882   NY: Ogilvie, People's Library.
1929   L/NY: OUP World's Classics no 343.
1981   NY: Arno Press, 2 vols, intro J. Hillis Miller.
1987   L: OUP World's Classics, ed Julian Thompson.

64. THE DUKE'S CHILDREN

Written: 2 May - 29 October 1876.
MS: Yale University, New Haven, Connecticut (Beinecke Library).
Serialised: All the Year Round, 4 Oct 1879 - 24 Jul 1880, vols 43-5.
Book publication:
1880   Chapman & Hall, 3 vols; in 1 vol Select Library of Fiction no 417 same year.
        NY: Munro, Seaside Library.
        NY: Harper, Franklin Square Library no 126.
        Leipzig: Tauchnitz, 3 vols.
        St Petersburg (Russian - **Asti Gerzoga**).
1881   L: Ward Lock, Select Library of Fiction no 29.
        Budapest: Naplo (Hungarian - **A Herceg Gyermekei**).
1893   NY: Dodd, Mead, 3 vols; further issue 1903.
1902   Philadelphia: Gebbie, 3 vols, Collector's Edition vols 28-30.
1938   L/NY: OUP World's Classics, 2 vols nos. 462-3; in 1 vol 1946, 1951, 1957, 1963; intro C.B. Tinker 1971.
1954   L/NY/Toronto: OUP The Oxford Trollope, intro C.B. Tinker, ill Charles Mozley; reprinted 1973; paperback 1973.
1973   L: Panther Books, intro Simon Raven.
1984   L: OUP World's Classics, ed and intro Hermione Lee.
1991   N.Y: OUP intro Hermione Lee.
        L: Trollope Society, intro Roy Jenkins.
        L: Folio Society: as above, ill L. Thomas.

65. THE LIFE OF CICERO

Written: 1st part 22 February - 12 March 1877.
MS: Princeton University, Princeton, New Jersey (Parrish Collection).
Book publication:
1880   L: Chapman & Hall, 2 vols.
1881   NY: Harper, 2 vols.
1981   NY: Arno Press, 2 vols, intro Ruth apRoberts.

66. DOCTOR WORTLE'S SCHOOL

Written: 8-29 April 1879.
MS: Yale University, New Haven, Connecticut (Beinecke Library).
Serialised: Blackwood's Magazine, May-Dec 1880, vols 127-8.
Book publication:
1880   NY: Harper, Franklin Square Library no 155.
1881   L: Chapman & Hall, 2 vols; in 1 vol same year.
        NY: Munro, Seaside Library.
        Arnhem: Rinken (Dutch - **De School van Dr. Wortle**).
        St Petersburg (Russian - **Shkola Rektora Vormlya**).
        Leipzig: Tauchnitz.
        L: Ward Lock, Select Library of Fiction no 20.
1928   L/NY: OUP World's Classics no 317; reprinted 1944, 1951, 1960.
1946   L: Pilot Press (with others, see item A94).
1984   L: OUP World's Classics, ed John Halperin.
1989   L: Trollope Society, intro John Rae.
        L: Folio Society, as above, ill R. Jacques.

67. AYALA'S ANGEL

Written: 25 April - 24 September 1878.
MS: Yale University, New Haven, Connecticut (Beinecke Library).
Serialised: Cincinnati Commercial, 6 Nov 1880 - 23 July 1881.
Book publication:
1881   L: Chapman & Hall, 3 vols; in 1 vol same year, 1882.
        NY: Harper, Franklin Square Library no 197.
        NY: Munro, Seaside Library.
        Leipzig: Tauchnitz, 3 vols.
1882   Moscow: 2 vols (Russian - **Angel Aglan**).
1884   L: Ward Lock, Select Library of Fiction no 30.
1890   Budapest: Nenzet (Hungarian - **Ayala Angyala**).
1898   St Petersburg: (Russian **Ayala Angel**).
1929   L/NY: OUP World's Classics no 342; reprinted 1960, 1968.

1964   L: OUP abridged Lord Hemingford, ill A.E.
Batchelor; reprinted 1966, 1967.
1986   L: OUP World's Classics, ed Julian
Thompson–Furnival.
1989   L: Trollope Society, intro A. Thomas Ellis.
L: Folio Society, as above, ill R. Geary.

68. WHY FRAU FROHMANN RAISED HER PRICES AND OTHER STORIES

Comprising *Why Frau Frohmann Raised Her Prices,
The Lady of Launay, Christmas at Thompson Hall,
The Telegraph Girl, Alice Dugdale.*
Book publication:
1882   L: Isbister [issued 1881]; in 2 vols 1883.
NY: Harper, Franklin Square Library no 248.
NY: Munro, Seaside Library.
L: Chatto & Windus, Piccadilly Library
(entitled **Frau Frohmann and Other
Stories**, fp Henry French; further issues
1884, 1892.
1883   Leipzig: Tauchnitz (omitting **Alice
Dugdale**).
1981   NY: Arno Press, intro Reginald Terry.

69. THE FIXED PERIOD

Written: 17 December 1880 - 28 February 1881.
MS: University of Michigan, Ann Arbor, Michigan
(Hatcher Library).
Serialised: Blackwood's Magazine, Oct 1881-Mar
1882, vols 130-1.
Book Publication:
1882   Edinburgh: Blackwood, 2 vols.
NY: Harper, Franklin Square Library no 239.
NY: Munro, Seaside Library.
Leipzig: Tauchnitz.
1981   NY: Arno Press, 2 vols, intro David Skilton.
1990   Ann Arbor: University of Michigan Press, ed
R.H. Super.

70. LORD PALMERSTON

Written: ?autumn/winter 1881.
MS: Princeton University, Princeton, New Jersey
(Taylor Collection).
Book publication:
1882   L: Isbister, English Political Leaders Series:
further issue 1883.
1981   NY: Arno Press, intro John Halperin.

71. MARION FAY

Written: 23 December 1878 - 21 November 1879.
MS: Princeton University, Princeton, New Jersey
(Taylor Collection).

Serialised: Graphic, 3 Dec 1881 - 3 Jun 1882, vols
24-5; Illustrated Sydney News; Vestnik Evropy, nos.
3-9, 1883 (Russian).
Book publication:
1882   L: Chapman & Hall, 3 vols.
NY: Harper, Franklin Square Library no 250.
NY: Munro, Seaside Library.
Leipzig: Tauchnitz, 2 vols.
1883   Christiana [Oslo]: Kriedt, 2 vols -
(Norwegian, **Marion Fay, eller den
Dodstomte**, trans W.S. Juell).
Russia: 2 vols (Russian - **Marion Fay**)
L: Chatto & Windus; further issues 1884,
1885, 1899.
1981   NY: Arno Press, 2 vols, intro Andrew
Wright.
1982   Ann Arbor: University of Michigan Press /
Racine, Wisconsin: Caledonia Press, intro
R.H. Super, ill William Small; re-issued in
paperback 1991.

72. KEPT IN THE DARK

Written: 18 August - 15 December 1880.
MS: University of Michigan, Ann Arbor, Michigan
(Hatcher Library).
Serialised: Good Words, May-Dec 1882, vol 23.
Book publication:
1882   L: Chatto & Windus, 2 vols, fp Millais; in 1
vol same year; Piccadilly Library 1884,
1891.
NY: Harper, Franklin Square Library no 272.
NY: Munro, Seaside Library.
Leipzig: Tauchnitz.
1883   Haarlem: Loosjes (Dutch - **In Het Duister
Gelaten**).
1978   NY: Dover Publications.
1987   Gloucester, England: Alan Sutton,
paperback.

73. THE TELEGRAPH GIRL

Magazine publication: Good Cheer, Christmas
number of Good Words 1877.
Book publication:
1882   NY: Ogilvie, People's Library.
1912   Berlin: Scherl (German/English - **Das
Telegraphenmädchen**).

74. THE TWO HEROINES OF PLUMPLINGTON

Magazine publication: Good Cheer, Christmas
number of Good Words 1882.
Book publication:
1883   NY: Munro, Seaside Library (with **Hagar, a
North Yorkshire Pastoral**, by Miss Linskill).

NY: Ogilvie, People's Library (with **Hagar**, as above).
1953 L: Andre Deutsch / NY: OUP [1954], intro John Hampden, ill Lynton Lamb.
1980 Racine, Wisconsin: Caledonia Press, intro John Kingsley Shannon.

75. NOT IF I KNOW IT

Magazine publication: Life, Christmas number 1882.
Book publication:
1883 NY: Munro, Seaside Library (with **Johnny's Christmas**, by B.C. Farjeon).

76. MR SCARBOROUGH'S FAMILY

Written: 14 March - 31 October 1881.
MS: Princeton University, Princeton, New Jersey (Taylor Collection).
Serialised: All the Year Round, 27 May 1882 - 16 Jun 1883, vols 49-52.
Book publication:
1883 L: Chatto & Windus, 3 vols; in 1 vol same year; Piccadilly Library 1885.
      NY: Harper, Franklin Square Library no 317.
      NY: J.W. Lovell.
      NY: Munro, Seaside Library.
      Hamburg: Richter, 3 vols, Asher's Library.
1886 NY: Dodd, Mead, Dollar Novels.
1946 L./NY: OUP World's Classics no 503; with intro James Pope-Hennessy 1973.
1984 Gloucester, England: Alan Sutton, intro Nicholas Mander.

77. ALICE DUGDALE AND OTHER STORIES

Comprising *Alice Dugdale, Aaron Trow, The O'Conors of Castle Conor, The Relics of General Chasse, The Chateau of Prince Polignac, George Walker at Suez.*
Book publication:
1883 Leipzig: Tauchnitz.
      NY: Munro, Seaside Library.
1885 Copenhagen: Mackeprang (Danish - **Skizzer og novelletter** trans and intro L. Kornelius).
1897 Budapest (Hungarian - **Dugdale Alice**).

78. LA MERE BAUCHE AND OTHER STORIES

Comprising *La Mère Bauche, John Bull on the Guadalquivir, Miss Sarah Jack of Spanish Town Jamaica, An Unprotected Female at the Pyramids, Mrs General Talboys.*
Book publication:
1883 Leipzig: Tauchnitz.
1884 NY: Munro, Seaside Library.

79. THE MISTLETOE BOUGH AND OTHER STORIES

Comprising *The Mistletoe Bough, The Courtship of Susan Bell, The Parson's Daughter of Oxney Colne, A Ride Across Palestine, The House of the Heine Brothers in Munich.*
Book publication:
1883 Leipzig: Tauchnitz.

80. AN AUTOBIOGRAPHY

Preface by Henry Merivale Trollope.
Written: October 1875 - 30 April 1876.
MS: British Library, London.
Book publication:
1883 Edinburgh: Blackwood, 2 vols; 2nd edn same year.
      NY: Harper; Franklin Square Library no 341 same year.
      NY: Lovell.
      NY: Munro, Seaside Library; pocket edn
1884 Leipzig: Tauchnitz.
1905 NY: Dodd, Mead; further issues 1911, 1922, 1935.
1923 L: OUP World's Classics no 239, intro Michael Sadleir; reprinted 1924, 1928, 1936; revised intro Michael Sadleir 1947, 1961, 1968.
1929 Oxford: Blackwell, Shakespeare Head Press.
1946 L: Williams & Norgate, intro Charles Morgan; reprinted in his **The Writer and His World** (L: Macmillan, 1960, pp 144-52).
1947 Berkeley: California University Press, intro Bradford A.Booth; reprinted 1978.
1950 L./NY/Toronto: OUP The Oxford Trollope, intro Frederick Page, ill from contemporary sources.
1960 NY: Doubleday Doran, Dolphin Books.
1962 L: Fontana, intro J.B. Priestley.
1980 L: OUP World's Classics, ed Michael Sadleir & Frederick Page, intro & notes P.D. Edwards.
1987 Gloucester, England: Alan Sutton.

81. THE LANDLEAGUERS

Written: June - December 1882; and unfinished - 49 chapters out of a projected 60 were completed.
MS: Princeton University, Princeton, New Jersey (Taylor Collection).
Serialised: Life [L], 16 Nov 1882 - 4 Oct 1883.
Book publication:
1883 L: Chatto & Windus, 3 vols, preliminary note and postscript by Henry Merivale Trollope; in 1 vol Piccadilly Novels, with postscript only 1885.
      NY: Munro, Seaside Library.

1885   Haarlem: Locajes, 2 vols (Dutch - **De Land-**
         Ligers, trans A.A. Deenik).
1979   NY: Garland, 3 vols, intro Robert Lee Wolff.
1981   NY: Arno Press, 3 vols, intro Robert Tracy.
1991   Gloucester, England: Alan Sutton.

82. AN OLD MAN'S LOVE

Written: 20 February - 9 May 1882.
MS: Princeton University, Princeton, New Jersey
(Taylor Collection).
Serialised: Izyashchnaya Literature 1884 (Russian -
Liubov Starova Cheloveka).
Book publication:
1884   Edinburgh: Blackwood, 2 vols.
         NY: Harper, Franklin Square Library no 373.
         NY: J.W. Lovell.
         NY: Munro, Seaside Library; also pocket
         edn.
         NY: N.L. Munro.
         Leipzig: Tauchnitz.
         Budapest: Egyertertes (Hungarian - **Egy**
         Oreg Ember Szerelme).
1885   NY: James B. Miller & Co.
         Arnhem: Quint (Dutch - **De Liefde van een**
         Ouden Vrijer).
1886   Budapest: Pesti Naplo (Hungarian - **Egy**
         Oreg Ember Szerelme).
1936   L/NY: OUP World's Classics no 444. In 1
         vol.
1981   NY: Arno Press, 2 vols, intro A.L. Rowse.
1984   Gloucester, England: Alan Sutton, intro
         Nicholas Mander.
1991   L: OUP World's Classics, ed John
         Sutherland.

83. THE COURTSHIP OF SUSAN BELL

Book publication:
1912   Stockholm: Bonnier (Swedish - trans O.P.
         Behm & F. Hjertberg).

84. THE NOBLE JILT

Written: 1850. A play in five acts. Never performed.
MS: University of Texas, Austin, Texas (Wrenn
Library).
Book publication:
1923   L: Constable, intro Michael Sadleir, limited
         to 500 copies.
1981   NY: Arno Press, with **Did He Steal It?**,
         foreword Robert H. Taylor.

85. THE O'CONORS OF CASTLE CONOR with AARON TROW

Book publication:
1924   L: Holerth Press.

86. LONDON TRADESMEN

Comprising *The Tailor, The Chemist, The Butcher,
The Plumber, The Horsedealer, The Publican, The
Fishmonger, The Greengrocer, The Wine Merchant,
The Coal Merchant, The Haberdasher.*
Serialised: Pall Mall Gazette Jul-Dec 1880.
Book publication:
1927   L: Elkin Mathews & Marrot / NY: Scribners,
         ed Michael Sadleir, limited to 530 copies;
         2nd edn 1928.
1970   NY: Kelly.

87. SHORT STORIES

Comprising *La Mère Bauche, The O'Conors of Castle
Conor, John Bull on the Guadalquivir, The Man Who
Kept His Money in a Box, The Two Generals,
Malachi's Cove.*
Book publication:
1928   L: Harrap, Short Stories of Today &
         Yesterday, intro F.H. Pritchard.

88. JOHN BULL ON THE GUADALQUIVIR

Book publication:
1928   Vienna: Steyermuhl (German/English -
         John Bull am Guadalquivir).

89. MALACHI'S COVE

Book publication:
1937   Edinburgh: Oliver & Boyd, Pleasure
         Readers, rewritten for children by Margaret
         E. Johnson, ill
1946   Ulm: Aegis-Verlag (German/English -
         Malachi's Bucht).
1948   Turin: G.B. Paravia (Italian - **Malachi's
         Cove**).
1953   Rome: A. Signoretti, with **The Verger** by W.
         Somerset Maugham.

90. THE TIRELESS TRAVELLER: TWENTY LETTERS TO THE LIVERPOOL MERCURY

Serial publication: Liverpool Mercury, 3 Jul-13 Nov
1875 [from Australia].
Book publication:

1941   Berkeley: University of California Press / L: Cambridge University Press, ed and intro Bradford A. Booth; paperback 1978.

91. THE MARRIAGE OF MARIE [La Mère Bauche]

Book publication:
1944   L: Polybooks, fp Frank R. Grey, paperbound, pp 16.

92. LETTER FROM ANTHONY TROLLOPE DESCRIBING A VISIT TO CALIFORNIA 1875

MS: Huntington Library, San Marino, California.
Serial publication: Huntington Library Quarterly, Oct 1939.
Book publication:
1946   San Francisco: Colt Press, wood engravings Malette Dean, limited to 500 copies.

93. THREE TALES

Comprising *The Chateau of Prince Polignac, The O'Conors of Castle Conor, The Relics of General Chasse.*
Book publication:
1946   Paris: Didier, The Rainbow Library, ed Louis Rocher; further issue 1948.

94. NOVELS AND STORIES

Comprising *Barchester Towers, Malachi's Cove, The Turkish Bath, Mary Gresley, Father Giles of Ballymoy, Dr Wortle's School.*
Book publication:
1946   L: Pilot Press, intro John Hampden, ill Joan Hassall; reprinted 1947, 1949.

95. CHRISTMAS DAY AT KIRKBY COTTAGE

Serial publication: Routledge's Christmas Annual 1870.
Book publication:
1947   L: Sampson Low, intro William Spode, ill Joan Hassall, "A Greetings Book", bound in stiff paper and designed to be sent as a postal package.

96. THE PARSON'S DAUGHTER AND OTHER STORIES

Comprising *The Parson's Daughter of Oxney Colne,*

La Mère Bauche, Father Giles of Ballymoy, The Spotted Dog, Alice Dugdale.
Book publication:
1949   L: Folio Society, intro John Hampden, ill Joan Hassall.

97. THE SPOTTED DOG AND OTHER STORIES

Comprising *The Spotted Dog, The Courtship of Susan Bell, Father Giles of Ballymoy, La Mère Bauche, The O'Conors of Castle Conor, Malachi's Cove, An Unprotected Female at the Pyramids.*
Book publication:
1950   L: Pan Books, ed Herbert van Thal.

97A. THE LETTERS OF ANTHONY TROLLOPE

Book publication
1951   L/NY: OUP ed Bradford A. Booth
1983   Stanford: Stanford Universuty Press, ed N. John Hall and Nina Bergis (completely revised).

98. MARY GRESLEY AND OTHER STORIES

Comprising *The O'Conors of Castle Conor, The Journey to Panama, *Katchen's Caprices, The Turkish Bath, Mary Gresley.*
Book publication:
1951   L: Folio Society, intro John Hampden, ill Joan Hassall.
1974   Philadelphia: Folcroft.

(*Attributed to Anthony Trollope in error. **Katchen's Caprices**, first published in All the Year Round, and in Harper's Magazine (22 Dec 1866-12 Jan 1867) was almost certainly written by Frances Eleanor Trollope.)

99. THE JOURNEY TO PANAMA & MALACHI'S COVE

Book publication:
1951   Berlin: Georg Westermann.

100. PRAESTENS DATTER I OXNEY COLNE [The Parson's Daughter of Oxney Colne]

Book publication:
!964   Copenhagen: Hasselbalch, trans and intro H.M. Berg (Danish).

101. NEVER, NEVER - NEVER, NEVER

Serialised: Sheets for the Cradle [Boston, ed Susan Hale], 6,8 and 10 Dec 1875.
Book publication:
1971   L: privately printed, The Valley Press, ed and intro Lance O. Tingay, limited to 25 copies.

102. THE NEW ZEALANDER

Written: 1855-6.
MS: Princeton University, Princeton, New Jersey (Taylor Collection).
Publication:
1972   Oxford: Clarendon Press, ed and intro N. John Hall.

103. THE PALLISERS

An abridgement of **Can You Forgive Her?**, **Phineas Finn**, **The Eustace Diamonds**, **Phineas Redux**, **The Prime Minister**, **The Duke's Children**.
Book publication:
1974   L: Weidenfeld & Nicolson, abridged and intro Michael Hardwick; also issued as paperback.
1975   NY: Coward, MacCann & Geoghegan.

104. WHY FRAU FROHMANN RAISED HER PRICES

Serialised: Good Words, Feb-May 1877.
Book publication:
1978   Racine, Wisconsin: Caledonia Press.

105. THE COMPLETE SHORT STORIES: VOLUME 1: THE CHRISTMAS STORIES

Comprising *The Mistletoe Bough, Christmas at Thompson Hall, Christmas Day at Kirkby Cottage, The Two Heroines of Plumplington, The Widow's Mite, The Two Generals, Catherine Carmichael, Not If I Know It.*
Book publication:
1979   Fort Worth, Texas: Texas Christian University Press, ed and intro Betty Jane Breyer.
1990   L: Pickering & Chatto.

106. THE COMPLETE SHORT STORIES: VOLUME II: EDITORS AND WRITERS

Comprising *The Turkish Bath, Mary Gresley, The Panjandrum, Mrs General Talboys, The Spotted Dog, Mrs Brumby, The Misfortunes of Fred Pickering,*

Josephine de Montmorenci.
Book publication:
1979   Fort Worth, Texas: Texas Christian University Press, ed and intro Betty Jane Breyer.
1990   L: Pickering & Chatto.

107. ALICE DUGDALE

Serial publication: Good Cheer, Christmas number Good Words 1878.
Book publication:
1980   Racine, Wis: Caledonia Press.

108. THE COMPLETE SHORT STORIES: VOLUME III: TOURISTS AND COLONIALS

Comprising *Miss Sarah Jack of Spanish Town Jamaica, The Man Who Kept His Money in a Box, An Unprotected Female at the Pyramids, Relics of General Chassé, The Banks of the Jordan, John Bull on the Guadalquivir, The Chateau of Prince Polignac, George Walker at Suez, Aaron Trow, Returning Home.*
Book publication:
1981   Fort Worth, Texas: Texas Christian University Press, ed and intro Betty Jane Breyer.
1990   L: Pickering & Chatto.

109. THE TWO HEROINES OF PLUMPLINGTON AND OTHER STORIES

Comprising *The Two Heroines of Plumplington, Why Frau Frohmann Raised Her Prices, John Bull on the Guadalquivir, Malachi's Cove, Aaron Trow, The Man Who Kept His Money in a Box, Lotta Schmidt, Christmas at Thompson Hall.*
Book publication:
1981   L: Folio Society, selected Herbert van Thal, intro Julian Symons, ill Peter Reddick.

110. MISCELLANEOUS ESSAYS AND REVIEWS

Comprising his contributions to Dublin University Magazine, Cornhill, St James's Magazine, Fortnightly Review, Transactions of the National Association for the Promotion of Social Science, Blackwood's Magazine, Good Words, Nineteenth Century and North American Review.
Book publication:
1981   NY: Arno Press, intro Michael Y. Mason.

111. WRITINGS FOR SAINT PAUL'S MAGAZINE

Comprising 19 essays, 2 reviews
Book publication:
1981   NY: Arno Press, intro John Sutherland.

112. COLLECTED SHORT STORIES

Comprising *The Gentle Euphemia, Katchen's Caprices*, Christmas Day at Kirkby Cottage, Never, Never - Never, Never, Catherine Carmichael, The Two Heroines of Plumplington, Not if I Know It.*
Book publication:
1981   NY: Arno Press, intro Susan L. Humphries.
(* Attribution to A.T. in error. See item A98).

113. THE BARCHESTER CHRONICLES

An abridgement of **The Warden, Barchester Towers, Doctor Thorne, Framley Parsonage** and **The Last Chronicle of Barset**.
Book publication:
1982   L: Futura Macdonald, abridged and ed Michael Hardwick.

114. THE COMPLETE SHORT STORIES: VOLUME IV: COURTSHIP AND MARRIAGE

Comprising *The O'Conors of Castle Conor, The Parson's Daughter of Oxney Colne, Malachi's Cove, The Telegraph Girl, Alice Dugdale, The Courtship of Susan Bell, Miss Ophelia Gledd, The Lady of Launay.*
Book publication:
1982   Fort Worth, Texas: Texas Christian University Press, ed and intro Betty Jane Breyer.
1991   L: Pickering & Chatto.

115. THE COMPLETE SHORT STORIES: VOLUME V: VARIOUS STORIES

Comprising *Why Frau Frohmann Raised Her Prices, Lotta Schmidt, Father Giles of Ballymoy, The Last American Who Left Venice, The House of the Heine Brothers in Munich, La Mère Bauche, The Gentle Euphemia, The Journey to Panama.*
Book publication:
1983   Fort Worth, Texas: Texas Christian University Press, ed and intro Betty Jane Breyer.
1991   L: Pickering & Chatto.

116. THE SPOTTED DOG AND OTHER STORIES

Comprising *The Spotted Dog, The Turkish Bath, Mary Gresley, Josephine de Montmorenci, The Panjandrum, Mrs Brumby.*
Book publication:
1983   Gloucester, England: Alan Sutton, intro Nicholas Mander.

117. AN UNPROTECTED FEMALE AT THE PYRAMIDS AND OTHER STORIES

Comprising *An Unprotected Female at the Pyramids, The O'Conors of Castle Conor, The Mistletoe Bough, The Parson's Daughter of Oxney Colne, The Courtship of Susan Bell.*
Book publication:
1984   Gloucester, England: Alan Sutton, intro Nicholas Mander.

118. MALACHI'S COVE & OTHER STORIES & ESSAYS

Comprising *Malachi's Cove, Father Giles of Ballymoy, La Mère Bauche, The Journey to Panama, Miss Ophelia Gledd;* essays, 'Charles Dickens', 'A Walk in a Wood'.
Book publication:
1985   Padstow, Cornwall, England: Tabb House, intro & notes Richard Mullen.

119. THE IRISH FAMINE: SIX LETTERS TO THE EXAMINER 1849/1850

Book publication:
1987   L: The Silverbridge Press, ed Lance O. Tingay.

120. AN ILLUSTRATED AUTOBIOGRAPHY, INCLUDING HOW THE 'MASTIFFS' WENT TO ICELAND

Book publication:
1987   Gloucester, England: Alan Sutton, intro Joanna Trollope.

Section B: Uniform editions

1. 1858-84   British Authors, 90 vols (Leipzig: Tauchnitz) 45 Titles
2. 1862-77   Library of Select Fiction (NY: Harper) 12 Titles
3. 1866-80   Library of Select Fiction (L: Chapman & Hall) 27 Titles
4. 1871-75   L/NY: Routledge 18 Titles
5. 1878-79   The Chronicles of Barsetshire, 8 vols (L: Chapman & Hall) 6 Titles
6. 1879-84   Franklin Square Library (NY: Harper) 16 Titles
7. 1879-85   Piccadilly Novels (L: Chatto & Windus) 7 Titles
8. 1880-84   Select Library of Fiction (L: Ward Lock) 30 Titles
9. 1881-84   Seaside Library (NY Munro) 46 Titles
10. 1883-85   Popular Works (L: Chatto & Windus) 9 Titles
11. 1892-1912   NY: Dodd, Mead, 42 vols 18 Titles
12. 1900-2   The Collector's Edition (Philadelphia: Gebbie) the Barset & Parliamentary series, 30 vols, 250 copies only 12 Titles
13. 1902-6   New Pocket Library, (L/NY: Lane) 16 vols 13 Titles
14. 1904-9   L: Routledge / NY: Dutton, the Barset series 6 Titles
15. 1906-11   L: Bell / NY: Macmillan, the Barset series, **Phineas Finn** & **Phineas Redux**, 12 vols 8 Titles
16. 1907-29   Everyman's Library (L: Dent / NY: Dutton) the Barset series, **The Golden Lion of Granpère** & **Phineas Finn**, 10 vols 8 Titles
17. 1907-48   The World's Classics (L: OUP) 38 Titles
18. 1913-4   New Century Library (L: Nelson), the Barset series; issued as Nelson's Classics 1917-48 6 Titles
19. 1925   L: Hayes, the Barset series (a re-issue of the Routledge series 1904-09) 6 Titles
20. 1928   L: Lane, the Bodley Head, the Barset series, 8 vols 6 Titles

21. 1928   Shakespeare Head Press (Oxford: Blackwell), the Barset series & **An Autobiography**, 14 vols, 525 copies only. 7 Titles
22. 1948-54   The Oxford Crown Trollope (L/NY/Toronto: OUP), the Parliamentary Letters series, **An Autobiography**, **The Warden** & **Barchester Towers**, 16 vols. The Parliamentary series were re-issued in 6 vols in 1975, hardback & paperback. 9 Titles
23. 1950-52   The Borzoi Trollope (NY: Knopf) 4 Titles
24. 1951-52   Oslo: Mortensen, the Barset series omitting **The Warden** (Norwegian), 10 vols. 5 Titles
25. 1967-72   Penguin English Library (L: Penguin Books). 5 Titles
26. 1973   L: Panther Books, the Parliamentary series. 6 Titles
27. 1976-80   L: Folio Society, the Barset series.6 Titles
28. 1977-85   NY: Dover Publications. 12 Titles
29. 1978-80   Harting Grange Library (Racine, Wisconsin: Caledonia Press) 5 Titles
30. 1979   NY: Garland, 14 Vols. 5 Titles
31. 1979   Complete Short Stories (Texas Christian University Press) Ed with intro Betty Jane Breyer.42 Titles
32. 1980-85   The World's Classics (L: OUP). To 1991: 33 Titles
33. 1981   NY: Arno Press, Selected Works of Anthony Trollope, 62 vols. Facsimiles of the 1st editions. 36 Titles
34. 1989   Trollope Society. Original illustrations reproduced from 1st editions. To 1991: 12 Titles
35. 1989   Folio Society. Joint edn with Trollope Society, all with newillustrations. To 1991: 12 Titles
36. 1990-91   Complete Short Stories. Pickering & Chatto / Trollope Society. With intro Betty Jane Breyer, foreword Joanna Trollope. 42 Titles

Section C: Short Stories

1. RELICS OF GENERAL CHASSE

1860	Harper's Magazine *20* 363-70 (Feb).
1861	Item A12.
1883	Item A77.
1885	Item A77 (Danish translation).
1946	Item A93.
1981	Item A108.

2. THE O'CONORS OF CASTLE CONOR

1860	Harper's Magazine *20* 799-806 (May).
1861	Item 12.
1875	In *Treasure Trove* series, vol 2 ed W.S. Walsh.
[1875?]	In *Half Hours with Great Novelists* (Chicago).
1883	Item A77.
1885	Item A77 (Danish translation).
1924	Item A85.
1928	Item A87.
1930	In *Great English Short Stories*, ed Lewis Melville & R. Hargreaves (NY: Viking)
1946	Item A93.
1950	Item A97.
1982	Item A114.
1984	Item A117.

3. THE COURTSHIP OF SUSAN BELL

1860	Harper's Magazine *21* 366-78 (Aug).
1861	Item 12.
1883	Item A79.
1912	Item A83 (Swedish translation)
1950	Item A97.
1958	In *Outstanding Short Stories*, simplified and abridged G.C. Thornley (L: Longman).
1982	Item A114.
1984	Item A117.

4. AN UNPROTECTED FEMALE AT THE PYRAMIDS

1860	Cassell's Illustrated Family Paper 6-13 (Oct).
1861	Item A12.
1883	Item A78.
1950	Item A97.
1981	Item A108.
1984	Item A117.

5. THE CHATEAU OF PRINCE POLIGNAC

1860	Cassell's Illustrated Family Paper 20-27 (Oct).
1861	Item A12.
1883	Item A77.
1885	Item A77 (Danish translation).
1946	Item A93.
1981	Item A108.

6. MISS SARAH JACK OF SPANISH TOWN JAMAICA

1860	Cassell's Illustrated Family Paper 3-10 (Nov).
1861	Item A12.
1883	Item A78.
1981	Item A108.

7. JOHN BULL ON THE GUADALQUIVIR

1860	Cassell's Illustrated Family Paper 17-24 (Nov).
1861	Item A12.
1883	Item A78.
1884	Nadlindatel' (Russian translation).
1928	Items 84-85 (German translation).
1944	In *Great Stories of the Nineteenth Century, 1st Series* (Paris: Didier, Rainbow Library).
1981	Items A108 - A109.

8. THE BANKS OF THE JORDAN; A RIDE ACROSS PALESTINE

1861	London Review *5* (12 and 19 Jan).
1863	Item A16, as 'A Ride Across Palestine'.
1883	Item A79, as 'A Ride Across Palestine'.
1981	Item A108.

9. MRS GENERAL TALBOYS

1861	London Review (2 Feb).
1863	Item A16.
1883	Item A78.
1896	In *Tales by English Authors* (NY: Scribners).
1979	Item A106.

10. THE PARSON'S DAUGHTER OF OXNEY COLNE

1861	London Review (2 Mar).
1863	Item A16.
1883	Item A79.
1964	Item A100 (Danish translation)
1982	Item A114.
1984	Item A117.

11. THE MAN WHO KEPT HIS MONEY IN A BOX

1861	Public Opinion (2-9 Nov) Literary Supplement.
1863	Item A16.
1888	Chemodan Z Den'gami (Russian translation).
1928	Item A87.
1981	Items A108 - A109.

12. THE HOUSE OF THE HEINE BROTHERS IN MUNICH

1861	Public Opinion (16-23 Nov) Literary Supplement.
1863	Item A16.
1883	Item A79.
1983	Item A115.

13. RETURNING HOME

1861	Public Opinion 30 Nov Literary Supplement; 7 Dec 234-6.
1863	Item A16.
1981	Item A108.

14. AARON TROW

1861	Public Opinion 14 and 21 Dec, 266-8 and 302-4.
1863	Item A16.
1883	Item A77.
1885	Item A77 (Danish translation).
1924	Item A85.
1981	Items A108 - A109.

15. THE MISTLETOE BOUGH

1861	Illustrated London Review Christmas Supplement (21 Dec).
1863	Item A16.
1883	Item A77.
1979	Item A105.
1984	Item A117.

16. GEORGE WALKER AT SUEZ

1861	Public Opinion, (28 Dec).
1863	Item A16.
1883	Item A77.
1885	Item A77 (Danish translation).
1981	Item A108.

17. THE JOURNEY TO PANAMA

1861	In *Victoria Regia*. ed Adelaide A. Proctor (L: Emily Faithfull & Co.) pp187-214.
1867	Item A31.
1927	In *English Short Stories, Third Series* (L: OUP World's Classics).
[1927?]	In *The Big Book of Great Short Stories*, ed H. Douglas Thomson & G. Clark Ramsay (L: Odhams).
1949	In *Short Stories of the Past*, ed C.H. Lockitt (L: Longman).
1951	Items A98 - 9.
1983	Item A115.
1985	Item A118.

18. LA MERE BAUCHE

1861	Item A12.
1883	Item A78.
1927	In *English Short Stories, Third Series* (L: OUP World's Classics).
1928	Item A87.
1940	In *Great English Short Stories, Volume 2*, ed J. Hampden (L: Pelican Books).
1944	Item A91.
1949	Item A96.
1950	Item A97.
1972	In *Loves and Deaths*, ed Peter Bayley (L: OUP).
1983	Item A115.
1985	Item A118.

19. THE WIDOW'S MITE

1863	Good Words 33-43 (Jan).
1867	Item A31.
1979	Item A105.

20. THE TWO GENERALS

1863	Good Words 853-61 (Dec).
1867	Item A31.
1928	Item A87.
1979	Item A105.

21. MISS OPHELIA GLEDD

1863	In *A Welcome* (L: Emily Faithfull & Co.) pp 239-83.
1867	Item A31.
1982	Item A114.
1985	Item A118.

22. MALACHI'S COVE

1864	Good Words 829-36 (Dec).
1865	Littell's Living Age *84* 35-44 (Jan).
1867	Item A31.
1867	Bibliothèque Universelle et Revue Suisse, vol 29 (French - *Le Baie Malachi*).
1875	In *Tales, Travels, Plays, Selected from Asher's Collection, volume 4*, ed Chr. Bauch (Berlin: Engelmann).
[1875?]	Riga: Latvian translation.
1914	In *English Short Stories, Nineteenth Century*, ed Hugh Walker (L:Milford, World's Classics).
1917	In *Book of Narratives*, ed O.J. Campbell & R.A. Rice (NY: Heath).
1923	In *Masterpiece Library of Short Stories, Volume 8* ed J.A. Hammerton (L: Educational Book Co.)
1928	Item A87.
1930	In *Short Stories of Yesterday*, ed F.H. Pritchard (US: Crofts).
1932	In *Selected English Stories, Volume 2*, ed J. Hampden (L: Macmillan).
1934	In *A Century of Thrillers*, preface James Agate (L: Daily Express).
1937	Item A89.
	In *Short Stories Retold, Book I*, ed H.A. Treble (L: OUP).
1940	In *Bedside Book of Famous British Stories*, intro Bliss Perry, ed B.A. Cerf & H.C. Moriarty (NY: Random House).
1946	Item A89 (German translation).
	Item A94.
1948	Item A89 (Italian translation).
1950	Item A97.
1951	Item A99.
1953	Item A89.
1958	In *Short Stories of the Nineteenth Century*, ed J.G. Fyfe (L: Blackie).
1972	In *Loves and Deaths*, ed Peter Bayley (L: OUP).
1981	Item A109.
1983	Item A115.
1985	Item A118.

23. FATHER GILES OF BALLYMOY

1866	Argosy *1* 511-23 (May).
1867	Item A31.

1946	Item A94.
1949	Item A96.
1950	Item A97.
1983	Item A115.
1985	Item A118.

24. THE GENTLE EUPHEMIA

1866	Fortnightly Review *4* 692-9 (1 May).
1981	Item A112.
1983	Item A115.

25. LOTTA SCHMIDT

1866	Argosy *2* 130-46 (Jul).
	Bibliothèque Universelle et Revue Suisse, vol 26 (French translation).
1867	Item A31.
[1867?]	In *World's Great Stories of Love and Romance* (L: Odhams).
1981	Item A109.
1983	Item A115.

26. THE ADVENTURES OF FRED PICKERING

1866	Argosy *2* 292-306 (Sep) entitled *The Misfortunes of Fred Pickering*.
1867	Item A31.
1979	Item A106.

27. THE LAST AMERICAN WHO LEFT VENICE

1867	Good Words Jan 50-8.
	Item A31.
1983	Item A115.

28. THE TURKISH BATH

1869	Saint Paul's Magazine *5* 110-28 (Oct).
	Galaxy *8* 689-703 (Nov).
	Littell's Living Age *103* 807-17 (Dec).
1870	Item A40.
1946	Item A94.
1951	Item A98.
1979	Item A106.
1984	Item A116.

29. MARY GRESLEY

1869	Saint Paul's Magazine *5* 237-56 (Dec).
1870	Item A40.
1946	Item A98.

1979   Item A106.

30. JOSEPHINE DE MONTMORENCI

1869   Saint Paul's Magazine 5 366-84 (Dec).
        Galaxy 8 825-39 (Dec).
1870   Item A40.
1979   Item A106.
1984   Item A116.

31. THE PANJANDRUM

1870   Saint Paul's Magazine, 5 434-53 (Jan) and
        562-77 (Feb).
        Galaxy Feb-Mar.
        Item A40.
1979   Item 106.

32. THE SPOTTED DOG

1870   Saint Paul's Magazine 5 669-88 (Mar) 6
        58-77 (Apr).
        Galaxy 9 497-511 (Apr) 611-25.(May).
        Littell's Living Age 105 272-83 (Apr)
        355-66 (May).
        Item A40.
1949   Item A96.
1950   Item A97.
1979   Item A106.

33. MRS BRUMBY

1870   Saint Paul's Magazine 6 180-99 (May).
        Item A40.
1979   Item A106.
1984   Item A114.

34. CHRISTMAS DAY AT KIRKBY COTTAGE

1870   Routledge's Christmas Annual 1870, pp 1-
        25.
1938   In *A Cabinet of Gems,* ed Bradford
        A. Booth (Berkeley: University of
        California Press).
1947   Item A95.
1948   In *A Fireside Book of Yuletide Tales.*
        ed E. Wagenknecht (Indianapolis:
        Bobbs Merrill).
1979   Item A105.
1981   Item A112.

35. NEVER, NEVER - NEVER, NEVER

1875   Sheets for the Cradle [Boston], 6, 8 and 10
        Dec.

1971   Item A101.
1981   Item A112.

36. CHRISTMAS AT THOMPSON HALL

1876   Graphic, Christmas Number.
1877   Item A54.
1882   Item A68.
1885   Item A54.
1891   Item A54.
1894   Item A54.
1901   Item A54.
1912   Item A54.
1979   Item A54.
1979   Item A105.

37. WHY FRAU FROHMANNN RAISED HER PRICES

1877   Good Words Feb-May.
1883   Item A68.
1978   Item A104.
1981   Item A109.
1983   Item A115.

38. THE TELEGRAPH GIRL

1877   Good Words, Christmas Number of Good
        Words, pp 1-19.
1882   Items A68 and A73.
1912   Item A73.
1982   Item A114.

39. THE LADY OF LAUNAY

1878   Light [L:], in 6 weekly numbers 6 Apr-11
        May and in 2 monthly numbers May-Jun.
        Item A59.
1882   Item A68.
1982   Item A114.

40. ALICE DUGDALE

1878   Good Cheer, Christmas Number of Good
        Words, pp 1-31.
1882   Item A68.
1883   Item A77.
1885   Item A77 (Danish translation).
1949   Item A96.
1978   Item A107.
1982   Item A114.

41. CATHERINE CARMICHAEL

1878   Masonic Magazine, Christmas Number,
        pp 2-16.
1979   Item A105.
1981   Item A112.

42. NOT IF I KNOW IT

1882   Life, Christmas Number, pp 45-8.
1883   Item A75.
1979   Item A105.
1981   Item A112.

**43. THE TWO HEROINES OF
OF PLUMPLINGTON**

1882   Good Cheer, Christmas Number of Good
        Words, pp 1-32.
        Harper's Bazaar, Dec
1883   Item A74
1953   Item A74
1979   Item A105
1981   Item A109

Section D: Periodical writings other than fiction

1. ATHENAEUM

1862   2 Sep, 22 Oct: letters on 'American
        Literary Piracy'.
        6 Dec, 730-1; 27 Dec, 848: letters
        defending T.A. Trollope's Lenten Journey
        in Umbria.
1863   3 Jan, 24; 10 Jan 60: letters defending T.A.
        Trollope's Lenten Journey in Umbria.

2. BLACKWOOD'S MAGAZINE

1877   *121* 597-604 (May): 'Whist at Our Club'*;
        reprinted in *Tales from Blackwood's* (n.s.
        12) 1881, pp 102-22.

3. CORNHILL MAGAZINE

1861   *3* 214-28 (Feb): article 'The Civil Service as
        a Profession'.*
1864   *9* 134-7 (Feb): article 'W.M. Thackeray';*
        reprinted in Theodore Taylor [ps. of John
        Cotton], *Thackeray: the Humorist and
        the Man of Letters* (NY: Appleton, 1864), in
        US edns only.

4. THE DAILY TELEGRAPH

1869   1 Apr: letter on his political characters.
1871   23 Dec: letter-article on Australia.
1872   13 Feb, 13 Mar, 2 Oct, 9 Oct, 10 Oct, 17
        Oct, 23 Oct, 29 Oct, 24 Dec, 28 Dec: letter-
        articles on Australia, signed 'Antipodean'.
        6 Aug: letter on the play *Shilly Shally*.

5. DUBLIN UNIVERSITY MAGAZINE

1851   May: review Merivale *History of the
        Romans* (vols I-II).*
1855   Oct: article 'The Civil Service'.*
1856   Jul: review Merivale's *History of the
        Romans* (vols IV-V).*

6. EXAMINER

1849   25 Aug, 532-3: letter-article 'Irish Distress'.
1850   30 Mar, 201; 6 Apr, 217; 11 May, 297-8; 1
        Jun, 346; 15 Jun, 377-8: letter-articles 'The
        Real State of Ireland'.

7. FORTNIGHTLY REVIEW

1865   *1* 129-46 (1 Jun) review Henry Taylor's
        Poems.
        1 491-8 (1 Jul) article 'Anonymous
        Literature'.*
        1 633-5 (15 Jul) review Ruskin's *Sesame
        and Lilies.*
        2 82-90 (15 Aug) article 'The Irish
        Church'.*
        2 255-6 (1 Sep) review Hannay's
        Characters and Criticism.
        2 379-80 (15 Sep) review Baker's *The Day
        and the Hour.*
        2 476-86 (1 Oct) article 'Public Schools'.*
        2 613-26 (15 Oct) article 'The Civil
        Service'.*
1866   *3* 529-38 (15 Jan) article 'The Fourth
        Commandment'* / *3* 650-2, review
        Buxton's *Ideas of the Day on Policy.*
        3 775-7 (1 Feb) review Alberto Mario's
        The Red Shirt.

4 510-2 (1 Apr) review Hutton's *Studies in Parliament.**
5 126-8 (15 May) review Sir M. Peto's *Resources and Prosperity in America.**
5 251-4 (1 Jun) review Goldwin Smith's *Civil War in America.**
5 381-4 (15 Jun) review Ruskin's *Crown of Wild Olives.**
6 632-6 (1 Nov) review Harriet Parr's *Life and Death of Jeanne d'Arc.**

1867　*7* 252-5 (Feb) review Mrs Sewell's *Rose of Cheriton;** reprinted in issue of Mar 1953.

1869　*11* 748-50 (Jun) review Hooper's *Flood, Field and Forest;** reprinted in issue of Aug 1953.
12 616-25 (Dec) article 'Mr Freeman and the Morality of Hunting'.*

1877　*27* 594-515 (Apr) article 'Cicero as a Politician'.*
28 401-22 (Sep) article 'Cicero as a Man of Letters'.*

1878　*29* 191-206 (Feb) article 'The Kaffir Land'.*
30 175-90 (Aug) article 'Iceland';* reprinted as pamphlet same year – see item A57.

1879　*31* 15-24 (Jan) article 'George Henry Lewes';* reprinted in Littell's Living Age, Feb, 149:307-13.

8. GOOD WORDS

1877　May, 377-84: article 'The Young Women at the London Telegraph Office'.*

1879　Feb, 98-105: essay 'In the Hunting Field'.*
Sep, 595-600: essay 'A Walk in a Wood';* reprinted in Appleton's Journal *7* 452-7 (Nov).

9. LIVERPOOL MERCURY

1875　3 Jul, 10 Jul, 17 Jul, 24 Jul, 31 Jul, 7 Aug, 14 Aug, 21 Aug, 28 Aug, 4 Sep, 11 Sep, 18 Sep, 25 Sep, 2 Oct, 9 Oct, 12 Oct, 23 Oct, 30 Oct, 6 Nov, 13 Nov: letter-articles on Australia. They were also printed in the Irish Times, the Aberdeen Free Press and the Kentish Express; reprinted in *The Tireless Traveller*, 1941 & 1978 (see item A90).

10. NEW YORK HERALD

1872　25 Nov: letter on A.T.'s rumoured law suit with Tauchnitz.

11. NINETEENTH CENTURY

1879　*5* 24-43 (Jan) essay 'Novel Reading: the Works of Dickens and Thackeray';* reprinted in Littell's Living Age, *140* 349-61 (Feb).

12. NORTH AMERICAN REVIEW

1879　*129* 203-22 (Sep) essay 'The Genius of Nathaniel Hawthorne'.*

1881　*132* 383-406 (Apr) essay 'Henry Wadsworth Longfellow'.*

13. NORTH BRITISH WEEKLY MAIL
[Glasgow] and others.

1877　Oct-Dec, letter-articles on South Africa; also in Aberdeen Daily Press, Cardiff Times, Glasgow Weekly Mail, Manchester Weekly Times, Northern Echo [Newcastle], Northern Whig [Belfast], Preston Guardian; Nov-Feb 1878 in Cape Times [Cape Town] and part publication in Eastern Star, Grocott's Penny Mail [Grahamstown], Observer [Port Elizabeth], Queenstown Representative.

14. PALL MALL GAZETTE

1865　7 Feb, letter-article 'The American Question'.
9 Feb, essay 'The Man Who Hunts and Doesn't Like It'.**
10 Feb, 'The Man Who Hunts and Does Like It'.
17 Feb, essay 'The Lady Who Rides to Hounds'.**
23 Feb, essay 'The Hunting Farmer'.**
25 Feb, letter-article 'England and America'.
28 Feb, letter 'Ladies in the Hunting Field'.
2 Mar, review 'The Public School Calendar 1865'.
7 Mar, essay 'The Man Who Hunts and Never Jumps'.**
11 Mar, essay 'The Hunting Parson'.**
15 Mar, essay 'The Master of the Hounds'.**
16 Mar, letter-article 'The American Conflict'.
20 Mar, letter-article 'Accusations against Lord Brougham'.
20 Mar, essay 'How to Ride to Hounds'.**
23 Mar, letter-article 'Usurers and Clerks in Public Offices'.

28 Mar, letter-article 'What is a Job? – 1'.
6 Apr, letter-article 'The American War'.
12 Apr, letter-article 'The Election of
M. Paradol to the French Academy'.
17 Apr, letter-article on St. Alban incident
in the American Civil War.
5 May, letter-article on the assassination
of Lincoln.
8 May, letter-article 'What is a Job? – 2'.
10 May, article 'A Zulu in Search of a
Religion'.
2 Jun, letter on the American Seccession.
28 Jun, letter-article 'What is a Job? – 3'.
27 Jul, letter-article 'The Civil Service'.
3 Aug, essay 'The Family that Goes
Abroad because it's the Thing to Do'.***
7 Aug, essay 'The Man who Travels
Alone'.***
10 Aug, essay 'The Unprotected Female
Tourist'.***
14 Aug, essay 'The United Englishmen
Who Travel for Fun'.***
22 Aug, essay 'The Art Tourist'.***
29 Aug, essay 'The Tourist in Search of
Knowledge'.***
2 Sep, essay 'The Alpine Club Man'.***
6 Sep, essay 'Tourists Who Don't Like
Their Travels'.***
11 Sep, letter-article 'Anglican
Sisterhoods'.
20 Nov, essay 'The Modern English
Archbishop'.†
27 Nov, essay 'English Bishops, Old and
New'.†
2 Dec, essay 'The Normal Dean of the
Present Day'.†
11 Dec, essay 'The Archdeacon'.†
18 Dec, essay 'The Parson of the Parish'.†
29 Dec, essay 'The Town Incumbent'.†

1866 5 Jan, essay 'The College Fellow Who Has
Taken Orders'.†
8 Jan, letter-article on England and the
U.S.A.
20 Jan, essay 'The Curate in a Popular
Parish'.†
23 Jan, essay 'The Irish Beneficed
Clergyman'†
25 Jan, essay 'The Clergyman Who
Subscribes for Colenso'.†
5 Feb, letter-article 'The Sabbath
Question'.
18 Jul, letter-article on Lord Russell
and the Saturday Review.
24 Jul, letter-article 'Curate's
Incomes'.

1867 13 Apr, article on Robert Bell.
16 May, letter 'Irish Prison Fare'.

1868 31 Mar, letter-article 'Copyright
in England and America'.
15 Jun, letter-article on impeachment of
the U.S. President.
11 Jul, letter-article 'The United
States'.

1869 21 May, letter on A.T.'s rumoured lawsuit
with Tauchnitz.

1872 16 Jul, letter on the play *Shilly Shally*.

1880 10 Jul, essay 'The Tailor'.††
17 Jul, essay 'The Chemist'.††
24 Jul, essay 'The Butcher'.††
29 Jul, essay 'The Plumber'.††
5 Aug, essay 'The Horse Dealer'.††
11 Aug, essay 'The Publican'.††
18 Aug, essay 'The Fishmonger'.††
23 Aug, essay 'The Greengrocer'.††
26 Aug, essay 'The Wine Merchant'.††
28 Aug, essay 'The Coal Merchant'.††
7 Sep, essay 'The Haberdasher'.††

15. PARLIAMENTARY PAPERS

1857 'History of the Post Office in Ireland', 56-
63, Appendix J in *Third Report of the
Postmaster General* (London, HMSO)

16. ST JAMES'S MAGAZINE

1861 2:163-76 (Sep): article 'The National
Gallery'.*

17. SAINT PAUL'S MAGAZINE

1867 *1* 1-7 (Oct) introduction to new magazine
1 76–91 (Oct) article 'On Sovereignty'.
1 206-19 (Nov) essay 'About Hunting'. †††
1 292-305 (Dec) essay 'An Essay on
Carlylism'.

1868 *1* 419-24 (Jan) article 'The Uncontrolled
Ruffianism of London'.
1 531-45 (Feb) article 'Whom Shall We
Make Leader of the New House of
Commons?'.
1 675-90 (Mar) essay 'About Hunting'. †††
2 147-60 (May) article 'The Irish Church
Debate'.
2 662-75 (Sep) article 'American
Reconstruction'.
3 163-72 (Nov) review E.S. Dallas's edition
of Richardson's *Clarissa*.

1869 *3* 538-51 (Feb) article 'The New Cabinet
and What It Will Do for Us'.
3 663-75 (Mar) article 'President Johnson's
Last Message'.
4 192-7 (May) article 'Mr Disraeli and the
Mint'.
4 450-55 (Aug) article 'The Irish Church
Bill in the Lords'.
5 75-80 (Oct) review of the play *Formosa*.

5 214 (Nov) editorial comment as postscript
to essay 'In Babyland'.‡
5 286-301 (Dec) article 'What Does Ireland
Want?'.

1870   5 620-30 (Mar) article 'Mr Gladstone's
Irish Land Bill' / 5 664-8, review *Ancient
Classics for English Readers.*
6 370-5 (Jul) obituary of Charles Dickens;
reprinted in Eclectic Magazine, Sep, *n s. 12*
297-301 (Sep 1870) and in Dickensian,
1910.
6:447-51 (Aug) article 'Mr Disraeli and the
Dukes'.
6 562-71 (Sep) article 'The English Aspect
of the War'.

18. THE TIMES

1874   24 Sep, 28 Sep, 27 Nov, 10 Dec: letters
complaining of train service to Basle.

19. TRANSACTIONS OF THE NATIONAL ASSOCIATION FOR THE PROMOTION OF SOCIAL SCIENCES

1867   *10* 119-25: article 'On the Best Means
of Extending and Securing an International
law of copyright.*

Notes

*	Reprinted in **Miscellaneous Essays and Reviews**, 1981 (item A110).
**	Reprinted in **Hunting Sketches**, 1865 (item A22).
***	Reprinted in **Travelling Sketches**, 1866 (item A26).
†	Reprinted in **Clergymen of the Church of England**, 1866 (item A27).
††	Reprinted in **London Tradesmen**, 1927 (item A86).
†††	reprinted in **British Sports and Pastimes**, 1868 (item A34).
‡	Omitted from **Writings from St. Paul's Magazine** (item A111).

PART TWO
Books and articles about Anthony Trollope

The following list, arranged by year, is not intended to be exhaustive. For the period of AT's lifetime and through to 1884, all significant reviews of his works that could be discovered have been included, but a great many biographical notes, newspaper reports which happen to mention AT, and controversial articles – such as disputes about field sports – have been omitted. From 1885 to 1990, and especially for more recent times, the coverage is less inclusive, only books and articles which are wholly or mainly about AT being listed. Readers in search of more comprehensive coverage are referred to to Mary Leslie Irwin, *Anthony Trollope, a bibliography* (New York, 1926; facsimile reprint, New York, 1968) for work on AT up to 1925, and to John Charles Olmsted and Jeffrey Egan Welch, *The reputation of Anthony Trollope, an annotated bibliography 1925 -1975* (New York and London, 1978).

The order of the article, within each year, is roughly as follows: general studies or articles which deal with more than one work, followed by reviews of individual books by AT, the books listed in the order (so far as is known) in which they were published within the year. Reviews are listed in chronological order of appearance, with articles in monthly magazines recorded after weekly or daily papers. Volume numbers of magazines are in italic (those for references to *Athenaeum* are for issue numbers), followed by page numbers in roman.

PART TWO
Books and articles about Anthony Trollope

1847

The Macdermots of Ballycloran (pbd May)
Critic 5 344 (1 May)
Spectator 20 449 (8 May)
[H.F. Chorley], *Athenaeum 1020* 517 (15 May)
John Bull 27 327 (22 May)
Douglas Jerrold's Weekly Newspaper 2 9 May, 661
Douglas Jerrold's Shilling Magazine 5 566 (Jun)
Essentially the same review, but omitting a long extract from the book
Howitt's Journal of Literature and Popular Progress 1 350 (19 Jun)
New Monthly Magazine n.s. 80 249 (Jun)

1848

The Kellys and the O'Kellys (pbd 27 Jun)
[H.F. Chorley], *Athenaeum 1081* 701 (15 Jul)
Douglas Jerrold's Weekly Newspaper 22 Jul, 941
New Monthly Magazine n.s. 83 544 (Aug)
Sharpe's London Magazine 7 118-21 (Aug)
The Times 7 Sep, 6

1850

La Vendée (pbd Jun)
Examiner 15 Jun. 373-4
[H.F. Chorley], *Athenaeum 1184* 708 (6 Jul)

1855

The Warden (pbd 20 Dec 1854)
Examiner 6 Jan, 5
Spectator 28 27-8 (6 Jan)
[Geraldine Jewsbury], *Athenaeum 1422* 107-8 (27 Jan)
Leader 6 164-5 (17 Feb)
Eclectic Review n.s. 9 359-61 (Mar)

1857

Barchester Towers (pbd May)
Examiner 16 May, 308
Spectator 30 525-6 (16 May)
Leader 8 497 (23 May)
[H. St. John], *Athenaeum 1544* 689-90 (30 May)
Saturday Review 3 503-4 (30 May)
Eclectic Review n.s. 2 54-9 (Jul)
[E.S. Dallas], *The Times* 13 Aug, 5
[George Meredith], *Westminster Review n.s. 12* 594-6 (Oct)

The Three Clerks (pbd 30 Nov)
Saturday Review 4 517-18 (5 Dec)
Spectator 30 1300-1 (12 Dec)
Examiner 19 Dec, 803-4
Leader 8 1218 (19 Dec)
[Geraldine Jewsbury], *Athenaeum 1574* 1621 (26 Dec)

1858

[Richard Holt Hutton?] 'Mr Trollope's Novels'. *National Review 7* 416-35 (Oct). On *The Warden*, *Barchester Towers*, *The Three Clerks* and *Doctor Thorne*

Barchester Towers (1857)
National Review 7 416-35 (Oct)
Emile Montegut, 'Le roman des moeurs en Angleterre', *Revue des deux mondes 2nd ser,* 17 756-8 (Oct)

Doctor Thorne (pbd May)
Examiner 29 May, 340
Leader 9 519-20 (29 May)
Spectator 31 577-8 (29 May)
[Geraldine Jewsbury], *Athenaeum 1597* 719 (5 Jun)
Saturday Review 5 618-19 (12 Jun)
Harper's Magazine 17 693 (Sep)

1859

The Bertrams (pbd Mar)
Spectator 32 328-9 (19 Mar)
[Geraldine Jewsbury], *Athenaeum 1639* 420 (26 Mar)
Illustrated London News 34 308 (26 Mar)
Saturday Review 7 368-9 (26 Mar)
Examiner 2 Apr, 212
Leader 10 431 (2 Apr)
[E.S. Dallas], *The Times* 23 May, 12
Bentley's Quarterly Review 1 456-62 (Jul)
National Review 9 187-99 (Jul)
New Monthly Magazine 115 500 (Jul)

The West Indies and the Spanish Main (pbd Nov)
[H. St. John], *Athenaeum 1671* 591-3 (5 Nov)
Spectator 32 1166-7 (12 Nov)
Saturday Review 8 643-5 (26 Nov); and 8 675-6 (3 Dec). First article reprinted in *Littell's Living Age 64* 209-12 (28 Jan 1860)

1860

E.D. Forgues, 'Romans de la vie anglaise', *Revue des deux mondes, 2nd ser.* 29, 369-98. Reviews *The Bertrams* and *Castle Richmond*

The Three Clerks (1857)
Harper's Magazine 21 261 (Jul)
American Theological Review 2 553-4 (Aug)

The West Indies and the Spanish Main (1859)
[E.S. Dallas], *The Times* 6 Jan, 4, and 18 Jan, 12
British Quarterly Review 31 263 (Jan), and 32 98-122 (Jul)
North American Review 90 289 (Jan)
Harper's Magazine 21 260-1 (Jul)
Quarterly Review 108 103ff. (Oct)

Castle Richmond (pbd 10 May)
[Geraldine Jewsbury], *Athenaeum 1699* 681-2 (19 May)
Saturday Review 9 643-4 (19 May)
Spectator 33 477 (19 May)
British Quarterly Review 32 233-4 (Jul)
Harper's Magazine 21 410 (Aug)

1861

Orley Farm (pt 1)
[W.H. Dixon], *Athenaeum 1741* 319-20 (9 Mar)

Framley Parsonage (serialised Jan 1860 to Apr 1861; in book form Apr 1861)
[W.H. Dixon], *Athenaeum 1747* 528 (20 Apr)
Examiner 20 Apr. 244-5
Saturday Review 11 451-2 (4 May)
London Review 2 544-5 (11 May)
British Quarterly Review 34 263 (Jul)
Eclectic Review 8th ser., 1 126-8 (Jul)
'J.A.', *Sharpe's London Magazine n.s. 19* 103-5 (Jul)
Westminster Review n.s. 20 282-4 (Jul)
American Theological Review 3 765 (Oct)

Tales of all countries (pbd Nov)
Saturday Review 12 587-8 (Dec)

1862

Framley Parsonage (1861)
Dublin University Magazine 59 405-6 (April)

Tales of all countries (1861)
Spectator 35 80 (18 Jan)

North America (pbd May)
[W.H. Dixon], *Athenaeum 1804* 685-7 (24 May)
Saturday Review 13 625-6 (31 May)
Spectator 35 635-6 (7 Jun)

[S. Lucas], *The Times* 11 Jun, 6
Chambers' Journal 3rd ser. 17 408-9 (28 Jun)
[G.H. Lewes or Frederick Greenwood], *Cornhill 6* 105-7 (Jul)
Dublin University Magazine 60 75-82 (Jul)
Harper's Magazine 25 262-3 (Jul)
[D.C. Lathbury, *Home and Foreign Review 1* 111-28 (Jul)
Presbyterian Quarterly Review 11 173 (Jul)
Fraser's Magazine 66 256-64 (Aug)
[E.B. Hamley], *Blackwood's Magazine 92* 372-90 (Sep)
British Quarterly Review 36 477 (Oct)
J.R. Cooke, *North American Review 95* 416-36 (Oct)
[Robert Cecil}, 'The Confederate struggle and recognition', *Quarterly Review 112* 53570 (Oct). On *North America* and five other works

Orley Farm (serialised Mar 1861 to Oct 1862; in book form 3 Dec 1861 and 25 Sep 1862)
Spectator 35 5 (4 Jan). First volume only reviewed
[W.H. Dixon], *Athenaeum 1823* 425-6 (Oct)
Saturday Review 14 444-5 (11 Oct)
[Richard Holt Hutton?], *Spectator 33* 1136-8 (11 Oct)
London Review 5 344-5 (18 Oct)
Examiner 25 Oct, 677-8
'Mr Trollope and the lawyers', *London Review 5* 405-7 (8 Nov)
[G.H. Lewes, J.F.W. Herschel, or J.W. Kaye], *Cornhill 6* 702-4 (Nov)
[E.S. Dallas] *The Times* 26 Dec, 5

The Struggles of Brown, Jones and Robinson (serialised Aug 1861 to Mar 1862; not published separately in Britain until 1870)
American Theological Review 754
Harper's Magazine 25 115 (June)

1863

Orley Farm (1862)
Home and Foreign Review 2 291-4 (Jan)
National Magazine 13 48 (Jan)
National Review 16 27-40 (Jan)
[Alexander Smith], 'Novels and Novelists of the day', *North British Review 38* 168-90 (Feb). Notice of *Orley Farm* appears on 185-8
American Presbyterian Theological Review n.s. 1 361 (Apr)
Dublin University Magazine 61 437 (Apr)
Harper's Magazine 26 704 (Apr)

Tales of all Countries (second series) (pbd Feb)
Reader 1 224 (28 Feb)
Saturday Review 15 276-8 (28 Feb). Reprinted in *Littell's Living Age 76* 600-2 (28 March)
Spectator 36 20-1 (7 Mar)
National Review 16 522-5 (Apr)

Rachel Ray (pbd Oct)
[J.C. Jeaffreson], *Athenaeum 1877* 492-4 (17 Oct)
[E. Dicey?], *Reader 2* 437-8 (17 Oct)
Saturday Review 16 554-5 (24 Oct)
'Mr Trollope's caricature:– Rachel Ray', *Spectator 36* 2660-1 (24 Oct)
London Review 31 October, 467-8
[E.F. Dallas] *The Times* 25 December, 4

1864

[A.S. Kinnear], 'Mr Trollope's' novels', *North British Review n.s. 1* 369-401 (May)

Orley Farm (1862)
North British Review 40 369-401 (Jun)

Rachel Ray (1863)
American Presbyterian and Theological Review n.s. 2 185 (Jan)
Harper's Magazine 28 274 (Jan)
Westminster Review n.s. 25 291-3 (Jan)

The Small House at Allington (serialised Sep 1862 to Apr 1864; in book form Mar)
[J.C. Jeaffreson], *Athenaeum 1900* 437-8 (26 Mar)
Reader 3 418-9 (2 Apr)
Spectator 37 421-3 (9 Apr)
Illustrated London News 44 375 (16 Apr)
London Review 8 494-6 (7 May)
Saturday Review 17 595-6 (14 May)
North British Review 40 369-401 (Jun)
American Presbyterian and Theological Review n.s. 2 525-6 (Jul)
W.T. Washburn, *North American Review 99* 292-8 (Jul)
Westminster Review n.s. 26 251-2 (Jul)

1865

F.D.D'A. Planche, *The story of the Small House at Allington: a three volume novel epitomised.* (London, James Blackwood)

'The Fortnightly Review', *Reader 6* 35 (8 Jul). On Trollope's article 'On anonymous literature', in *Fortnightly Review,* 1 Jul 1865 (see D7)

'Mistaken estimates of self', *Saturday Review 19* 564 (13 May). On Trollope's letter on Lincoln's assassination in *Pall Mall Gazette,* 5 May 1865 (see D14)

Miss Mackenzie (pbd 28 Feb)
Saturday Review 19 263-5 (4 Mar)
Spectator 38 244-5 (4 Mar)
[Geraldine Jewsbury], *Athenaeum 1953* 455 (1 Apr)
London Review 10 387 (8 Apr)
Reader 5 596 (27 May)

Dublin University Magazine 65 576 (May)
Henry James, *Nation* (NY) *1* 51-2 (13 Jul)
Westminster Review n.s. 28 283-5 (Jul). Also reviews volume I of *Can You Forgive Her?*
[E.S. Dallas], *The Times* 23 Aug, 12

Hunting Sketches (pbd 10 May)
Spectator 37 587-8 (27 May)
Charles Stewart, *Fortnightly Review 1* 765-7 (1 Aug)
Reader 6 233 (26 Aug)

Can You Forgive Her? (serialised Jan 1864 to Aug 1865; in book form 1 Oct 1864 and Jun 1865)
Saturday Review 20 240-2 (19 Aug)
[Geraldine Jewsbury], *Athenaeum 1975* 305-6 (2 Sep)
Spectator 38 978-9 (2 Sep)
Henry James, *Nation* (NY) *1* 409-10 (28 Sep)
Month 3 319-23 (Sep)

1866

[Henry Alford], 'Mr Anthony Trollope and the English clergy', *Contemporary Review 2* 240-62 (Jun)

'An Amateur Theologian', *Saturday Review 21* 131-3 (3 Feb). On Trollope's article 'The Fourth Commandment' in *Fortnightly Review 3* 529-38 (see item D7)

The Belton Estate (serialised May 1865 to Jan 1866; in book form Dec 1865)
Henry James, *Nation* (NY) *2* 21-2 (4 Jan)
Spectator 3 103-4 (27 Jan)
['Wilberforce'], *Athenaeum 1997* 166 (3 Feb)
Saturday Review 21 140-2 (3 Feb)
London Review 12 260 (3 Mar)
Harper's Magazine 32 527 (Mar)
Contemporary Review 3 300-2

1867

Margaret Oliphant, *Blackwood's Magazine 102* 275-8 (Sep). On *The Claverings* and *The Last Chronicle of Barset.* Reprinted in *Littell's Living Age 95* 16-18 (5 Oct)
Saturday Review 24 11-12. On the death of Mrs Proudie
'Mr Trollope's New Magazine', *Spectator 40* 1120-1 (5 Oct). On *Saint Paul's Magazine*
Spectator 40 1219 (2 Nov). On AT's retirement from the Post Office

The Belton Estate (1866)
E.D. Forgues, 'Le roman anglais contemporain', *Revue des deux mondes 2nd ser. 69* 1017-8

Nina Balatka (serialised Jul 1866 to Jan 1867; in book form 1 Feb 1867)

[H.F. Chorley], *Athenaeum 2053* 288 (2 Mar)
London Review 14 266-7 (2 Mar)
[Richard Holt Hutton?] *Spectator 40* 329-30 (23 Mar)
Examiner 11 May, 293-4
Littell's Living Age 98 128 (11 Jul). From one of the London reviews

The Claverings (serialised Feb 1866 to May 1867; in book form 20 Apr 1867)
American Presbyterian and Theological Review n.s. 5 346 (Apr)
Spectator 40 498-9 (4 May). Reprinted in *Littell's Living Age 93* 779-82 (22 Jun)
London Review 14 547 (11 May)
Saturday Review 23 638-9 (17 May). Reprinted in *Littell's Living Age 93* 777-9 (22 Jun)
J. Knight, *Fortnightly Review n.s. 1* 770-72 (1 Jun)
[Geraldine Jewsbury], *Athenaeum 2068* 783 (15 Jun)
Harper's Magazine 36 128 (Dec)

The Last Chronicle of Barset (part issue 1 Dec 1866 to 6 Jul 1867; in book form Mar and Jul 1867)
Spectator 40 778-80 (13 Jul)
Examiner 20 Jul, 452-3
London Review 15 81 (20 Jul)
[Geraldine Jewsbury], *Athenaeum 2075* 141 (3 Aug)
British Quarterly Review 46 557-60 (Oct). Also reviews *Lotta Schmidt and other stories*
Harper's Magazine 36 128 (Dec)

Lotta Schmidt and other stories (pbd Aug 1867)
Saturday Review 24 381-2 (21 Sep)
Spectator 40 1062-3 (21 Sep)
[Geraldine Jewsbury], *Athenaeum 2091* 683-4 (23 Nov)

1868

The Claverings (1867)
S. Gorter, *De Gids 3* 171-84 (Jul). On the Dutch translation, pbd 1868

Linda Tressell (serialised Oct 1867 to May 1868; in book form May 1868)
Spectator 41 562-3 (9 May)
[J.C. Jeaffreson], *Athenaeum 2117* 724-5 (23 May)
Nation (NY) *6* 494-5 (18 Jun)
British Quarterly Review 48 281 (Jul)
Littell's Living Age 98 198 (Jul). From one of the London reviews

1869

'Mr Trollope's last Irish novel', *Dublin Review n.s. 13* 361-77 (Oct). On several of AT's Irish novels

J. Herbert Stack, 'Mr Anthony Trollope's Novels', *Fortnightly Review n.s. 5* 188-98 (1 Feb)

British Sports and Pastimes (pbd 7 Nov 1868)
Public Opinion 15 12 (2 Jan)
Spectator 43 16-17 (2 Jan)
Saturday Review 28 652-4 (13 Nov)

Phineas Finn (serialised Oct 1867 to May 1869; in book form Mar 1869)
Spectator 42 356-7 (20 Mar)
Saturday Review 27 431-2 (27 Mar)
Harper's Magazine 38 854 (May)
M.B., *Contemporary Review 12* 142-3
Dublin Review n.s. 13, 361-77

He Knew He Was Right (part issue 17 Oct 1868 to 22 May 1869; in book form May 1869)
Harper's Magazine 38 854 (May)
Saturday Review 27 751-3 (5 Jun)
Public Opinion 15 744 (12 Jun) and *16* 13 (3 Jul)
Spectator 42 706-8 (12 Jun)
[F.N. Broome], *The Times* 26 Aug, 4
British Quarterly Review 1 263-4 (Jul)

1870

'The parson of Mr Trollope's novels', *Every Saturday n.s. 1* 347-9 (28 May)

Phineas Finn (1869)
[W.B. Rands], *Contemporary Review 12* 142-3 (Jan)
De Gids Dec 546-7

The Vicar of Bullhampton (part issue Jul 1869 to May 1870; in book form Apr 1870)
['Collyer'], *Athenaeum, 2218* 574 (30 Apr)
[Margaret Oliphant], *Blackwood's Magazine 107* 647-8 (May). Also reviews *He Knew He Was Right*
Saturday Review 29 646-7 (14 May)
[George Dasent], *The Times* 3 Jun, 4
Harper's Magazine 41 459 (Aug)

An Editor's Tales (pbd May)
[John Doran], *Athenaeum 2230* 112 (23 Jul)
Public Opinion 18 199 (13 Aug)
Saturday Review 30 211-12 (13 Aug)
Graphic 2 183 (20 Aug)
[W.B. Rands], *Contemporary Review 15* 319 (Sep)
Spectator 43 1203 (8 Oct)
British Quarterly Review 52 542 (Oct)

The Commentaries of Caesar (pbd 1 Jun)
['Rumsey'], *Athenaeum 2224* 771 (11 Jun)
Spectator 43 757-8 (18 Jun)
[James Davies?], *Contemporary Review 15* 314 (Sep)

Sir Harry Hotspur of Humblethwaite (pbd Nov)
[George Dasent], *The Times* 16 Nov, 4
[Norman MacColl], *Athenaeum 2247* 654 (19 Nov)
Spectator 43 1415-16 (26 Nov)
Saturday Review 30 753-5 (10 Dec)

1871

The Struggles of Brown, Jones and Robinson (1862, in book form 1870)
British Quarterly Review 53 261-2 (Jan)
Westminster Review n.s. 39 574-5 (Apr)

Sir Harry Hotspur of Humblethwaite (1870)
Harper's Magazine 42 779-80 (Apr)

Ralph the Heir (part issue Jan 1870 to Jul 1871; in book form 6 Apr)
['Collyer'], *Athenaeum, 2268* 456 (15 Apr)
Spectator 44 450-3 (15 Apr)
[George Dasent], *The Times* 17 Apr, 6
Examiner 22 Apr, 419
Saturday Review 31 537-8 (29 Apr)
C.A. Bristed, *North American Review 112* 433-7 (Apr)
Graphic 3 418 (6 May)
British Quarterly Review 54 240-2 (Jul)
Harper's Magazine 43 458 (Aug)

1872

'The Novels of Mr Anthony Trollope', *Dublin Review n.s. 19* 393-430 (October)

The Golden Lion of Granpère (pbd May)
Spectator 45 630-1 (18 May)
['Collyer'] *Athenaeum 2326* 652-3 (25 May)
Saturday Review 33 833-5 (29 Jun)
Nation (NY) *15* 126 (22 Aug)
Harper's Magazine 45 624 (Sep)
Old and New 6 352 (Sep)

The Eustace Diamonds (serialised 1 Jul 1871 to 1 Feb 1873; in book form Dec 1872)
['Collyer'] *Athenaeum 2348* 527-8 (26 Oct)
Spectator 45 1365-6 (26 Oct)
[F.N. Broome], *The Times* 30 Oct, 4
Nation (NY) *15* 320 (14 Nov)
Saturday Review 34 637-8 (16 Nov)
Harper's Magazine 46 140 Dec

1873

Sir Harry Hotspur of Humblethwaite (1870)
J.H.C. Heijse, *De Gids* 181-88 (Jan)

Australia and New Zealand (1873)
[Sir Charles Wentworth Dilke], *Athenaeum 2366* 276 (1 Mar)
[F.N. Broome], *The Times* 12 Apr, 7
Saturday Review 35 554-5 (26 Apr)
British Quarterly Review 57 528-31 (Apr)
Spectator 46 607-8 and 640 (10 and 17 May)
Edith Simcox, *Fortnightly Review n.s. 13* 662-3

(May)
Richard Hengist Horne, *Contemporary Review 22* 699-730 (Oct)

1874

Phineas Redux (serialised 19 Jul 1873 to 10 Jan 1874; in book form Dec 1873)
Spectator 47 36-7 (3 Jan)
['Collyer'] *Athenaeum 2411* 53 (10 Jan)
Edith Simcox, *Academy 5* 141-3 (7 Feb)
Saturday Review 37 186-7 (7 Feb)
A.V. Dicey, *Nation* (NY) *18* 174-5 (12 Mar)
Harper's Magazine 49 135 (Jun)

The Way We Live Now (pt 1)
[Norman MacColl], *Athenaeum 2418* 291 (28 Feb)

Lady Anna (serialised Apr 1873 to Apr 1874; in book form May 1874)
[Norman MacColl], *Athenaeum 2424* 485 (11 Apr)
George Saintsbury, *Academy 5* 482 (2 May)
Saturday Review 37 598-9 (9 May)
Nation (NY) *19* 9-11 (2 Jul)
[George Dasent], *The Times* 24 Jul, 5
Harper's Magazine 49 290 (Jul)

Harry Heathcote of Gangoil (in *The Graphic* for 25 Dec 1873; in book form Oct 1874)
Harper's Magazine 48 747 (Apr)
['Collyer'] *Athenaeum 2454* 606 (7 Nov)
Saturday Review 38 609-10 (7 Nov)
George Saintsbury, *Academy 6* 652 (19 Dec)

1875

Harry Heathcote of Gangoil (1874)
British Quarterly Review 61 133 (Jan) and *62* 282 (Jul)
[Richard Holt Hutton] *Spectator 48* 247-8 (20 Feb)
F.M. Owen, *Academy 7* 396 (17 Apr)
Westminster Review n.s. 47 558 (Apr)

The Way We Live Now (part issue Feb 1874 to Sep 1875; in book form Jul 1875)
[Norman MacColl], *Athenaeum 2487* 851 (26 Jun)
[Meredith White Townsend] *Spectator 48* 825-6 (26 Jun)
Saturday Review 40 88-9 (17 Jul)
[Lady Barker], *The Times* 24 Aug, 4
Examiner 28 Aug, 384-5
Nation (NY) *21* 153-4 (2 Sep)
Harper's Magazine 51 754 (Oct)
Westminster Review n.s. 48 529-30 (Oct)

The Prime Minister (pt 1)
[Norman MacColl], *Athenaeum 2512* 829 (18 Dec)

The Prime Minister (serialised Nov 1875 to Jun 1876; in book form May 1876)
[Norman MacColl], *Athenaeum 2540* 15 (1 Jul)
Nation (NY) *23* 45-6 (20 Jul)
[Meredith White Townsend] *Spectator 49* 922-3 (22 Jul)
R.F. Littledale, *Academy 10* 106-7 (29 Jul)
[A.I. Shand], *The Times* 18 Aug, 4
Harper's Magazine 53 467-8 (Aug)
Saturday Review 42 481-2 (14 Oct)

1877

'The World of Fiction', *Church Quarterly Review 4* 136-62 (Apr)
'The character of Julius Caesar', *Dublin Review n.s. 28* 127-41 (Jan). On *The Commentaries of Caesar* (1870) and other works

[A.I. Shand], 'Mr Anthony Trollope's novels', *Edinburgh Review 146* 455-88 (Oct)

Thomas Chuck, *One story is good until another is told, or, A reply to Mr Anthony Trollope on that part of his work entitled* Australia and New Zealand, *relating to the colony of Victoria* (Liverpool, NSW)

Christmas at Thompson Hall (1876)
Harper's Magazine 55 149 (Jun)

The American Senator (serialised May 1876 to Jul 1877; in book form Jul 1877)
['Cook'] *Athenaeum 2590* 766-7 (16 Jun)
Saturday Review 43 803-4 (30 Jun)
Examiner 916-7 (21 Jul)
[A.I. Shand], *The Times* 10 Aug, 3
Nation (NY) *25* 122-3 (23 Aug)
Spectator 51 1101-2 (31 Aug)
Canadian Monthly 12 319-20 (Sep)
Harper's Magazine 55 790 (Oct)
[T.W. Crawley], *Academy 12* 487-8 (24 Nov)

1878

South Africa (pbd Mar)
[Frederick William Chesson?], *Athenaeum 2625* 211-12 (16 Feb)
Saturday Review 45 241-3 (23 Feb)
Coutts Trotter, *Academy 13* 294-6 (6 Apr)
Spectator 51 445 (6 Apr)
The Times 18 Apr, 7
[Henry Brackenbury], *Blackwood's Magazine 124* 100 (Jul)
British Quarterly Review 57 556-7 (Oct)
Church Quarterly Review 7 236-40 (Oct)

Is he Popenjoy? (serialised 13 Oct 1877 to 13 Jul 1878; in book form Apr 1878)

['Collyer'] *Athenaeum 2636* 567 (4 May)
Saturday Review 45 695-6 (1 Jun)
R.F. Littledale, *Academy 13* 505 (8 Jun)
Harper's Magazine 57 468 (Aug)
[A.I. Shand], *The Times* 14 Sep, 4
Spectator 51 1243-4 (5 Oct)

1879

G.M. Towle, 'A novelist of the day', *Appleton's Journal n.s.7* 275-8 (Sep)

'Trollope, Hawthorne, and the New Aestheticism', *Dublin University Magazine 4* 437-42 (Oct)

'Mr Trollope on the moral effect of novel–reading', *Spectator 52* 9-10 (4 Jan). On Trollope's article 'Novel–reading', *Nineteenth Century 6* 24-43 (Jan)

An Eye for an Eye (serialised 24 Aug 1878 to 1 Feb 1879; in book form Jan 1879)
['Collyer'] *Athenaeum 2672* 47 (11 Jan)
R.F. Littledale, *Academy 15* 117 (8 Feb)
Spectator 52 210-11 (15 Feb)
Saturday Review 47 410-11 (29 Mar)
Nation (NY) *28* 290 (24 Apr)

Thackeray (pbd May-Jun)
T.H. Ward, *Academy 15* 533 (21 Jun)
British Quarterly Review 70 247 (Jul)
Westminster Review n.s. 56 258 (Jul)
[W.B. Rands], *Contemporary Review 35* 768-9 (Jul)
Appleton's Journal n.s. 7 187-90 (Aug)
Fraser's Magazine n.s. 20 264-70 (Aug)
Harper's Magazine n.s. 59 474 (Aug)
Nation (NY) *29* 127-8 (Aug)
Scribner's monthly 18 632-3 (Aug)
Spectator 52 1130-2 (6 Sep)

John Caldigate (serialised Apr 1878 to Jun 1879; in book form Jun 1879
['Sergeant'] *Athenaeum 2694* 755 (14 Jan)
E. Purcell, *Academy 16* 5 (5 Jul)
Spectator 52 916-17 (19 Jul)
Examiner 2 Aug, 1000
[A.I. Shand], *The Times* 8 Aug, 3
Saturday Review 48 216-17 (16 Aug)
Harper's Magazine 59 631 (Sep)

Cousin Henry (serialised 8 Mar to 24 May; in book form Nov)
['Collyer'] *Athenaeum 2712* 495 (18 Oct)
Spectator 52 1319-21 (18 Oct)
Examiner 25 Oct, 1382
Saturday Review 48 515-16 (25 Oct)
William Wallace, *Academy 16* 316 (1 Nov)
[A.I. Shand], *The Times* 6 Nov, 6

1880

Harper's Magazine 60 314 (Jan). On *The Bertrams* and *Cousin Henry*

W.H. Bidwell, *Eclectic Magazine 94* 760-1 (Jun)

John Caldigate (1879)
Nineteenth Century 8 340 (Aug)

Thackeray (1879)
James Thomson, BV, *Cope's Tobacco Plant 2* 504 (Jul)

The Duke's Children (serialised 4 Oct 1879 to 24 Jul 1880; in book form Jun-Jul 1880)
['Cook'] *Athenaeum 2744* 694-5 (29 May)
Saturday Review 49 767-8 (12 Jun)
Spectator 53 755-6 (12 Jun)
Illustrated London News 76 622 (26 Jun)
A.G. Sedgwick, *Nation* (NY) *31* 138-9 (19 Aug)
Nineteenth Century 8 340 (Aug)
Harper's Magazine 61 643 (Sep)
Westminster Review n.s. 58 574 (Oct)

1881

The Life of Cicero (pbd late 1880)
Critic (NY) *1* 3-4 (29 Jan)
W. Warde Fowler, *Academy 19* 91-2 (5 Feb)
Saturday Review 51 279-80 (26 Feb)
[W. Lucas Collins], *Blackwood's Magazine 129* 211-28 (Feb)
[J. Clayton], *Spectator 54* 353-4 (12 Mar)
Springfield Republican [Massachusetts], 22 Mar
Harper's Magazine 62 791 (Apr)
Westminster Review n.s. 59 605-6 (Apr)
Nation (NY) *33* 75-6 (28 Jul)
['Piele'], *Athenaeum 2806* 170-71 (6 Aug)

Dr Wortle's School (serialised May to Dec 1880; in book form Jan 1881)
['Collyer'] *Athenaeum 2777* 93 (15 Jan)
Saturday Review 51 121-2 (22 Jan)
Critic (NY) *1* 35 (12 Feb)
Nation (NY) *32* 172-3 (10 Mar)
[A.I. Shand], *The Times* 16 Apr, 10
Harper's Magazine 62 636 (May)
Westminster Review n.s. 60 283-4 (Jul)

Ayala's Angel (Serialised 6 Nov 1880 to 23 Jul 1881; in book form Jun 1881)
['Cook'] *Athenaeum 2795* 686 (21 May)
Illustrated London News 78 526 (28 May)
Saturday Review 49 756-7 (11 Jun)
[E.A. Dillwyn], *Spectator 54* 804-5 (18 June)
[A.I. Shand], *The Times* 16 Jul, 10
Critic (NY) *1* 194 (16 Jul) and 218-9 (13 Aug)
Nation (NY) *33* 257 (29 Sep)

Harper's Magazine 63 794-5 (Oct)
Westminster Review n.s. 60 566-7 (Oct)

1882

Why Frau Frohmann raised her prices (pbd Dec 1881)
Arthur Baker, *Academy 21* 5 (7 Jan)
['Collyer'] *Athenaeum 2829* 54 (14 Jan)
Saturday Review 52 305-6 (11 Mar)
[R.H. Hutton], *Spectator 55* 443 (1 Apr)
Nation (NY) *34* 504-5 (15 Jun)
Critic (NY) *2* 201 (29 Jul)
Harper's Magazine 65 317 (Jul)

The Fixed Period (serialised Oct 1881 to Mar 1882; in book form Feb 1882)
['Collyer'] *Athenaeum 2837* 314-15 (11 Mar)
[R.H. Hutton], *Spectator 55* 360-1 (18 Mar)
Saturday Review 53 434-5 (8 Apr)
[A.I. Shand], *The Times* 12 Apr, 3-4
Nation (NY) *34* 385 (4 May)
Harper's Magazine 65 156 (Jun)
Westminster Review n.s. 62 285-6 (Jul)

Lord Palmerston (1882)
Academy 22 98-9 (5 Aug)
Saturday Review 54 182-3 (5 Aug)
['Henry R. Fox Bourne'] *Athenaeum 2864* 367 (16 Sep)
British Quarterly Review 76 450-1 (Oct)
Westminster Review n.s. 62 566 (Oct)

Marion Fay (serialised 3 Dec 1881 to 3 Jun 1882; in book form May 1862)
['Collyer'] *Athenaeum 2852* 793-4 (24 Jun)
Saturday Review 54 64-5 (8 Jul)
Nation (NY) *35* 78-9 (27 Jul)
Critic (NY) *2* 201 (29 Jul)
['Miss Lock'], *Spectator 55* 1088-9 (19 Aug)
Harper's Magazine 65 478 (Aug)

Kept in the Dark (serialised May to Dec 1882; in book form Aug or Sept 1882)
['Collyer'] *Athenaeum 2873* 658 (18 Nov)
W.E. Henley, *Academy 22* 377-8 (25 Nov)
Nation (NY) *35* 447-8 (23 Nov)
Graphic 26 710 (23 Dec)

Obituaries and summations
[Mary Augustus Ward], *The Times* 7 Dec, 9
Tribune (NY) 7 Dec, 2
['Henry R. Fox Bourne'] *Athenaeum 2876* 772-3 (9 Dec)
Saturday Review 54 755-6 (9 Dec)
[Richard Holt Hutton] *Spectator 55* 1573-4 (9 Dec)
R.F. Littledale, *Academy 22* 433 (16 Dec)
Graphic 26 661 (16 Dec)
Illustrated London News 81 618-9, 622 and 646 (16 Dec)

[Richard Holt Hutton] 'From Miss Austen to Mr Trollope' *Spectator 55* 1609-11 (16 Dec). Reprinted in *Littell's Living Age 156* 186-9 (20 Jan)
'Cuthbert Bede', 'Some Recollections of Mr Anthony Trollope', *Graphic 26* 707 (23 Dec)
Mowbray Morris, 'Anthony Trollope, a poem', *Graphic 26* 719 (30 Dec)
Literary World (Boston) *13* 456 (Dec)

1883

Obituaries and summations
Edward A. Freeman, 'Anthony Trollope', *Macmillan's Magazine 47* 236-40 (Jan). Reprinted in *Littell's Living Age 156* 177-81 (Jan) and *Eclectic Magazine 100* 406-10 (Mar)
James Bryce, 'The death of Anthony Trollope', *Nation* (NY) *36* 10-11 (Jan)
[Cecilia E. Meetkerke], 'Anthony Trollope', *Blackwood's Magazine 133* 316-20 (Feb)
'The Novels of Anthony Trollope' *Dublin Review 3rd series 9* 314-34 (Apr)
W.H. Pollock, 'Anthony Trollope', *Harper's Magazine 66* 907-12 (May)
Henry James, 'Anthony Trollope' *Century Magazine* (NY) *n.s. 4* 385-95 (Jul)
Margaret Oliphant, *Good Words* 142-4. Reprinted in *Littell's Living Age 156* 507-10 (Apr) and *Eclectic Magazine 100* 531-4 (Apr)

Lord Palmerston (1882)
Nation (NY) *36* 128-30 (Feb)

Kept in the Dark (1882)
['Miss Lock'], *Spectator 56* 88-9 (20 Jan)
British Quarterly Review 77 220-1 (Jan)
Harper's Magazine 66 317 (Jan)
Westminster Review n.s. 63 287 (Jan)

Mr Scarborough's family (serialised 27 May 1882 to 16 June 1883; in book form May 1883)
['Collyer'] *Athenaeum 2898* 600 (12 May)
[Meredith Townsend], *Spectator 56* 612-4 (12 May)
William Wallace, *Academy 23* 344 (19 May)
Saturday Review 55 642-3 (19 May)
Nation (NY) *36* 552-3 (28 Jun)
British Quarterly Review 78 233 (Jul)
Westminster Review n.s. 64 301 (Jul)
Harper's Magazine 67 479 (Aug)

An Autobiography (pbd Oct)
The Times 28 Sep, 3
The Times 12 and 13 Oct, 10 and 8
['Cook'] *Athenaeum 2920* 457-9 (13 Oct)
Graphic 28 391 (20 Oct)
Saturday Review 56 505-6 (20 Oct)
[Meredith Townsend], 'The boyhood of Anthony Trollope', *Spectator 56* 1343-4 (20 Oct)
Tribune (NY) 20 Oct, 4; and 23 Oct, 4

R.F. Littledale, *Academy 24* 273-4 (27 Oct)
[R.H. Hutton], 'Mr Trollope as critic', and 'Anthony Trollope's autobiography', *Spectator 56* 1373-4 and 1377-9 (27 Oct). Reprinted in *Littell's Living Age 159* 573-5 (1 Dec)
[W. Lucas Collins], *Blackwood's Magazine 134* 577-96 (Nov). Reprinted in *Littell's Living Age 159* 579-93 (8 Dec)
[John Morley and Mary Augusta Ward], *Macmillan's Magazine 49* 47-56 (Nov)
Contemporary Review 44 787 (Nov)
A.Tanzer, *Nation* (NY) *37* 396-7 (Nov)
Continent 4 736 and 768 (Dec)
[Henry Norman], 'Theories and Practice in Modern Fiction', *Fortnightly Review n.s. 34* 870-86 (Dec). (Review of *Autobiography* appears on 870-1)
Literary World 14 442-3 (Dec)
Julian Hawthorne, 'The maker of many books', *Manhattan 2* 573-8
Month 30 484-93

The Landleaguers (serialised 16 Nov 1882 to 4 Oct 1883; in book form Oct 1883)
E. Purcell, *Academy 34* 328 (17 Nov)
['Collyer'] *Athenaeum 2926* 666 (24 Nov)
Continent 2 605 and *4* 702 (Nov 1882 and Dec 1883)
[Rev. A.J. Church], *Spectator 56* 1627 (15 Dec)

1884

An Autobiography (1883)
British Quarterly Review 79 165-8 (Jan)
Critic (NY) *n.s. 1* 25-7 (19 Jan). Reprinted in *Littell's Living Age 160* 248-51 (26 Jan) and *Temple Bar 70* 129-34 (Jan)
[A.I. Shand], 'The literary life of Anthony Trollope', *Edinburgh Review 159* 186-212 (Jan) Reprinted in *Littell's Living Age 160* 451-65 (Feb)
'Sylvanus Urban', 'Trollope upon novel–writing', *Gentleman's Magazine 256* 100-1 (Jan)
Harper's Magazine 68 317 (Jan)
Westminster Review n.s. 65 83-115 (Jan). Reprinted in *Littell's Living Age 161* 195-212 (Apr)
Atlantic Monthly 53 267-71 (Feb)
Macmillan's Magazine 49 47-56 (Nov)
Marie Dronsart, 'Une Autobiographie du romancier Anthony Trollope', *Correspondant n.s. 101* 1111-34 (Dec)

The Landleaguers (1883)
Saturday Review 57 53-4 (12 Jan)
Westminster Review n.s. 65 276-7 (Jan)

An Old Man's Love (pbd Nov–Dec 1883)
C.E. Dawkins, *Academy 25* 220 (29 Mar)
Saturday Review 57 414-15 (29 Mar)
['Collyer'] *Athenaeum 2945* 438 (5 Apr)
[A.I. Shand], *The Times* 14 Apr, 3
British Quarterly Review 80 210-11 (Jul)

Julia Wedgwood, *Contemporary Review 46* 149-51 (Jul)
Harper's Magazine 69 318 (Jul)
Westminster Review n.s. 66 305 (Jul)

1885

'English character and manners as portrayed by Anthony Trollope', *Westminster Review n.s. 67* 53-100 (Jan). Reprinted in *Littell's Living Age 164* 478-503 (21 Feb)

1889

Margaret Oliphant, 'Success in fiction', *Forum 7* 314-22 (May). Reprinted in *Author* (Boston) *1* 70-2

1892

Edmund Yates, 'Personal traits of Anthony Trollope', *London world* 23 Feb

1894

Amelia B. Edwards, 'The art of the novelist', *Contemporary Review 66* 225-42 (Aug). Reprinted in *Littell's Living Age 202* 771-83 (22 Sep)

1895

Frederick Harrison, 'Anthony Trollope's place in literature', *Forum 19* 324-37 (May). Reprinted in his *Studies in early Victorian literature* (London, 1895)

1899

Richard Garnett, 'Anthony Trollope', *Dictionary of National Biography 57* 238-42

1900

Stephen Gwynn, *Macmillan's Magazine 81* 217-26

Anna B. McGill, 'Some famous literary clans: III. The Trollopes', *Book buyer 21* 195-203 (Oct)

1901

Walter F. Lord, 'The novels of Anthony Trollope', *Nineteenth century 49* 805-16 (May). Reprinted in Lord, *Mirror of the century* (London, 1906)

Leslie Stephen, *National Review 38* 68-84 (Sep). Reprinted in *Littell's Living Age 231* 366-78 (9 Nov) and *Eclectic Magazine 138* 112-24; and in Stephen, *Studies of a biographer*, vol IV (1902) 168-205

G.S. Street, *Cornhill 83* 349-55 (Mar). Reprinted in *Littell's Living Age Living Age 229* 128-33 (13 Apr); and in Street, *A book of essays* (1902) 198-212

1902

Gamaliel Bradford, *Atlantic Monthly 89* 426-32. Reprinted in Bradford, *A naturalist of souls* (1926) 135-54

1903

James Bryce, 'Merits and defects of Trollope', in *Studies in contemporary biography* (1903) 116-30

1904

Michael Macdonagh, 'In the throes of composition', *Cornhill n.s. 17* 607-27 (Nov). Reprinted in *Littell's Living Age 243* 776-91 (24 Dec)

1905

F.G. Bettany, 'In praise of Anthony Trollope's novels', *Fortnightly Review 83* 1000-11 (Jun). Reprinted in *Littell's Living Age 243* 166-76 (15 Jul)

Eugene W. Harter, 'The future of Trollope', *Bookman* (NY) *21* 137-41 (Apr)

1906

T.H.S. Escott, 'An appreciation and reminiscence of Anthony Trollope', *Fortnightly Review n.s. 80* 1096-1104 (Dec)

1909

T.H.S. Escott, *Quarterly Review 210* 210-30 (Jan). Reprinted in *Littell's Living Age 261* 459-72 (22 May)

1911

A. Edward Newton, *Trollopeana* (Daylesford, PA: privately printed). Suggesting the formation of a Trollope Society

1913

T.H.S. Escott, *Anthony Trollope: his work, associates and literary originals* (London/New York, John Lane). Also published under the title *Anthony Trollope: his public services, private friends and literary originals*. Reprinted 1973 (London / New York, Folcroft)

1919

Helen Bowen, 'Barsetshire and the war', *Atlantic Monthly 124* 286-7. A parody

1920

'Trollope and tea', *Atlantic Monthly 126* 134-6.

Sir Henry Chartres Biron, *National Review 75* 76-88. Reprinted in *Littell's Living Age 305* 165-175 (Apr) and in Biron, *Pious opinions* (London, 1923) 261-82

A. Edward Newton, 'A great Victorian', in *Amenities of book-collecting*, 249-66

W.L. Randell, 'Trollope and his work', *Fortnightly Review 114* 459-67 (Sep)

George Saintsbury, 'Trollope revisited', *Essays and studies 6* 41-66. Reprinted in *Collected Essays and Papers* vol II (1923)

1922

Ronald A. Knox, 'A ramble in Barsetshire', *London Mercury 5* 378-85 (Feb). With map

Michael Sadleir, *Excursions in Victorian bibliography* (London, Constable). Includes introductory essay on AT, first published as 'A guide to Anthony Trollope' in *Nineteenth century 91* 648 -58 (Apr 1922), and a list of first editions of AT's books

1924

Michael Sadleir, 'Why only Dickens?', *Nation and Athenaeum 34* 667-8 (9 Feb)

Michael Sadleir, 'A Trollope love story: Mary Thorne', *Nineteenth century 96* (Sep)

Michael Sadleir, 'Anthony Trollope and his publishers', *Library 4th ser. 5* 215-42 (Dec)

1925

E. Beresford Chancellor, 'Trollope and the Barsetshire novels', in *Literary Diversions* (London, Dulau), 113-20

D.M.J., 'Trollope's political novels', *TLS* 5 February, 88

Spencer van Bokkelen Nichols, *The significance of Anthony Trollope* (New York, McMurtrie)

George Henry Payne. 'Belle lettres in ballot boxes: a forgotten statesman, Plantagenet Palliser', *Forum 73*, 107-10 (Jan), 249-52 (Feb)

Michael Sadleir, 'The Victorian woman as Trollope drew her', in *Bermondsey Book 2* 14-22 (Mar)

1926

Rowland Greg, 'Anthony Trollope and his mother', *Cornhill n.s. 61* 557-64

Stephen Gwyn, 'Trollope and Ireland', *Contemporary Review 129* 72-9. Reprinted in *Littell's Living Age 328* 539-44

Mary Leslie Irwin, *Anthony Trollope, a bibliography* (New York): facsimile reprint New York, 1968. A reprint, with revisions, of articles in *Bulletin of Bibliography 12* (1925)

1927

F.J. Dunlop, 'Trollope in Russian', *TLS* 15 December, 961. On the Russian translation of *Is he Popenjoy?*

Sir Desmond MacCarthy, 'Notes on Trollope', *Empire Review*, March, 235-8. Reprinted in *Portraits* (New York, Putnam, 1931)

J.B. Priestley, 'In Barsetshire', *Saturday Review* 12 November, 658-9

Michael Sadleir, *Trollope: a commentary* (London, Constable)

1928

H.A.L. Fisher, 'The political novel', *Cornhill n.s. 64* 25-38. Compares AT and Disraeli

Paul Elmer More, 'My debt to Trollope' in *The demon of the absolute* (Princeton, Princeton University Press), 89-125

Michael Sadleir, *Trollope: a bibliography* (London, Constable). Reprinted London, Dawson, 1964, with *Addenda and corrigenda* (1934)

Hugh Walpole, *Anthony Trollope* (New York, Macmillan)

1929

M. Evangeline Bradhurst, 'Anthony Trollope – the hunting man. By one who remembers him', *Essex Review 38* 185-91

1930

'The Church of Trollope', *TLS* 13 February, 119

Clyde Furst, 'A new Trollope', *Saturday Review of Literature 6* 1005-7. In part a review of the Shakespeare Head edition of the Barsetshire novels

J. Penderel-Brodhurst, 'The Greater Trollope', *National Review 95* 420-8

1932

[H. Idris Bell], 'Anthony Trollope's *Autobiography*', *British Museum Quarterly 7* 72. On the purchase by the British Museum of the original MS of An Autobiography

Hilaire Belloc, 'Anthony Trollope', *London Mercury 27* 150-7

B.D. Cutler, 'The great Victorians come to America', *Publishers' Weekly*, 17 Dec, 2255-7. On the piracy of AT's novels by American publishers

Leonard Huxley, 'Anthony Trollope and the *Cornhill*', *Cornhill n.s. 73* 758-66

Edward F. Stephens, 'The Warden to the rescue', *Library Journal 57* 892-3. On text of *The Warden*

Hugh Walpole, 'Anthony Trollope', in *The great Victorians*, ed. H.J. Massingham, (London, Nicholson and Watson), 529-54

Arthur Waugh, 'Trollope after fifty years', *Fortnightly Review 138* 712-24

1933

Christiaan Conraad Koets, *Female characters in the works of Anthony Trollope* (Gouda, T. van Tilburg)

Wilfred Partington, 'Dickens, Thackeray and Yates: with an unknown 'indiscretion' by Trollope', *Saturday Review 155* 234-5. See also *Bookman 76* 206-8

1934

Lord David Cecil, 'Anthony Trollope', in *Early Victorian novelists: essays in revaluation* (London, Constable), 245-79

'E.', 'Anthony Trollope and the English drama', *Notes & Queries 167* 350. See also H.G. Dick, *Notes & Queries 180* (1941), 372-3

1935

Ronald A. Knox, *Barchester Pilgrimage* (London, Sheed and Ward). Imitation and continuation of the Barchester novels

1936

Stephen Gwynn, 'The return of Barchester', *Fortnightly Review 145* 108-10

1937

Ernest A. Baker, 'Trollope' in *The History of the English Novel* (London, Witherby), volume VIII, 112-60

Ashley Sampson, 'Trollope in the twentieth century', *London Mercury 35* 371-7

1938

Randolph G. Adams, 'The text of *Phineas Redux*', *Colophon n.s. 3* 460-1

1939

Harold Anson, 'The church in Nineteenth-century fiction III – Anthony Trollope', *Listener* 11 May, 998-9

Bradford A. Booth, 'Trollope in California', *Huntington Library Quarterly 3* 117-24. Publishes for the first time a sketch of California, from the original MS. See item A92

Henry James Wye Milley, '*The Eustace Diamonds* and *The Moonstone*', *Studies in Philology 36* 651-63. Proposes Collins's novel as a partial source for *The Eustace Diamonds*

1940

Francis X. Roellinger, 'E.S. Dallas in Trollope's *Autobiography*', *Modern Language Notes 55* 422-4
Michael Sadleir, 'A conundrum for Trollopians', *TLS* 19 October, 536. See also issues of 26 October, 548, and 2 November, 560

John Hazard Wildman, *Anthony Trollope's England* (Providence, Rhode Island, Brown University Press

1941

R.W. Chapman, 'The text of *Phineas Redux*', *Review of English Studies 17* 184-92. Answered by Gavin Bone, 'The text of *Phineas Redux:* a rejoinder', in same journal *17* 452-8

R.W. Chapman, 'The text of Trollope', *TLS* 25 January, 48, and 22 March, 144. See also Simon Nowell-Smith; *TLS* 8 February, 72, and R.W. Chapman, *TLS* 1 March, 108

R.W. Chapman, 'The text of Trollope's *Autobiography*', *Review of English Studies 17* 90-4

R.W. Chapman, 'The text of Trollope's novels', *Review of English Studies 17* 322-31

R.W. Chapman, 'Trollope's *American Senator*', *TLS* 21 June 304; and 12 July, 335

R.W. Chapman, 'The text of Trollope's *Autobiography*', *Notes & Queries* (181), 245

R.W. Chapman, 'Trollopian criticism', *TLS* 5 July, 232; and 26 July, 359

H.G. Dick, 'Queries from Anthony Trollope's notes on English drama' *Notes & Queries 180* 372-3. Reply by William Jaggard, same journal, 431. See also 1934 and 1959

Simon Nowell-Smith, 'Caldigate novels', *TLS* 22 November 579. See further Michael Sadleir, 20 December, 643; and Nowell-Smith, 3 January 1942, 7

W.M. Parker, 'Trollope's Scotland: his scenery in fact and fiction', *Scots Magazine,* August, 353-63

1942

Alban F.L. Bacon, 'The Trollope Mystery', *TLS* 22 August, 409

R.W. Chapman, 'A correction in Trollope', *TLS* 7 March, 116

R.W. Chapman, 'The text of Trollope's *Ayala's Angel*', *Modern Philology 39* 287-94

Christopher Hollis, 'The meaning of Anthony Trollope', in *For Hilaire Belloc: essays in honour of his 71st birthday*, (London/New York, Sheed and Ward), ed. Douglas Woodruff, 92-105

Michael Sadleir, 'A new Trollope item', *TLS* 25 July, 372. See also Charles Clay, *TLS* 8 August, 396; and Sadleir, *TLS* 29 August, 432

H.F. Summers, 'Trollope's *Phineas Redux*', *Review of English Studies 18* 228

Chauncey Brewster Tinker and R.W. Chapman, 'The text of Trollope's *Phineas Redux*', *Review of English Studies 18* 86-92

Allan Wade, 'The text of Trollope', *TLS* 10 January, 24. See also R.W. Chapman, *TLS* 10 January, 24; and Hope Emily Allen, *TLS* 4 April, 180

1943

R.W. Chapman, 'Akinetos', *Notes & Queries 185* 163

Harold Cooper, 'Trollope and Henry James in 1868', *Modern Language Notes 58* 558

J. T. , 'Trollope's apologia' *Notes & Queries 185* 105

1944

'Menander's mirror: imagining the future', *TLS* 9 Dec, 591

H. Oldfield Box, 'The decline and rise of Anthony Trollope', *Listener* 28 Dec, 718-9

R.W. Chapman, 'The text of Trollope's *Sir Harry Hotspur*', *Notes & Queries 186* 2-3

R.W. Chapman, 'The text of *Phineas Finn*', *TLS* 25 March 156. See also S. Nowell-Smith, *TLS* 15 April, 192, and R.L. Purdy, *TLS* 29 July, 372

C.L. Cline, '*Coningsby* and three Victorian novelists', *Notes & Queries 186* 41-2

T.C.D., 'Victorian editors and Victorian delicacy', *Notes & Queries 187* 251-3

Ralph Edwards, 'Trollope on Church affairs', *TLS* 21 October, 516. See also 'Fiction and fact', *TLS* 21 October, 511

Clement Greenberg, 'A Victorian novel', *Partisan*

Review 11 234-8. Reprinted in *Art and culture: critical essays* (Boston, Beacon Press, 1961). On *The American Senator*

Frank Pierce Jones, 'Anthony Trollope and the classics', *Classical Weekly 37* 227-31

1945

Bradford A. Booth, 'Preface', 'The Parrish Trollope collection', and 'Notes and Queries', and 'Notes and Queries', *The Trollopian* (later retitled *Nineteenth-century fiction*) *1* 1-4, 11-19 and 47-8

W. Bardsley Brash, 'The triumph of Anthony Trollope', *London Quarterly and Holborn Review 170* 293-9 (Jul)

R.W. Chapman, 'Textual criticism: a provisional bibliography', *Trollopian 1* 45

W.M. Parker, 'Anthony Trollope and 'Maga'', *Blackwood's Magazine 257* 57-64

K.S., 'Trollope in New Zealand', *Notes & Queries 189* 14

Michael Sadleir, 'Trollope and Bacon's Essays' *Trollopian 1* 21-34

Lucy Poate Stebbins and Richard Poate Stebbins, *The Trollopes: the chronicle of a writing family* (New York, Columbia University Press)

Richard Poate Stebbins, 'Trollope at Harrow School', *Trollopian 1* 44

C.J. Vincent, 'Trollope: a Victorian Augustan', *Queen's quarterly 52* 415-28

Frederic Connett White, 'Trollope's 'Roger Scratcherd'', *Notes & Queries 189* 129

Carroll A. Wilson, 'Morris L. Parrish: Trollope collector', *Trollopian 1* 5-10

1946

Ernest Boll, 'The infusion of Dickens in Trollope', *Nineteenth-century fiction 1* (September) 11-24

Elizabeth Bowen, *Anthony Trollope: a new judgement* (London/New York, Oxford University Press). A short play on the reputation of Trollope

Leo Mason, 'Dickens, Trollope and Joe Whelks', *Dickensian 42* 174-80. Compares Dickens and AT as suitable for dramatization

V.S. Pritchett, 'Trollope', *New Statesman n.s. 31* 415

Chauncey Brewster Tinker, 'Newton's Trollope Society', *Nineteenth-century fiction 1* (September) 1-3

John Hazard Wildman, 'About Trollope, in a postwar mood', *Nineteenth-century fiction 1* (March) 17-22

1947

Frderick G. Blair, 'Trollope on Education', *Nineteenth-century fiction 1* (March) 1-9

Bradford A. Booth, 'Trollope, Reade and 'Shilly Shally'', *Nineteenth-century fiction 1* (March) 45-54; and 2 43-51. On the production of and subsequent disputes about Reade's play, a dramatization of *Ralph the Heir*

Norris D. Hoyt, '*Can you forgive her?:* a commentary', *Nineteenth-century fiction 2* 57-50

Raymond Mortimer, *New Statesman n.s. 33* 277-8

Lionel Stevenson, 'Dickens and the origin of *The Warden*', *Nineteenth-century fiction 2* 83-9

Robert H. Taylor, 'The manuscript of Trollope's *The American Senator*', *Papers of the Bibliographical Society of America 41* 123-39

1948

Bradford A. Booth, 'Trollope and Little Dorrit'. *Nineteenth-century fiction 2* 237-40

R.W. Chapman, 'Personal names in Trollope's political novels', in *Essays mainly on the nineteenth century presented to Sir Humphrey Milford* (London, Oxford University Press), 72-81

Winifred Gregory Gerould and James Thayer Gerould, *A Guide to Trollope* (Princeton, Princeton University Press)

Frank E. Robbins, 'The ancient city of Barchester: a map', *Nineteenth-century fiction 3* 33

Robert H. Taylor, 'The Trollopes write to Bentley', *Nineteenth-century fiction 3* 83-98 and 201-14

Muriel R. Trollope, 'What I was told', *Nineteenth-century fiction 2* 223-35

1949

Bradford A. Booth, 'Trollope and the *Pall Mall Gazette*', *Nineteenth-century fiction 4* 51-69 and 137-58

R.W. Chapman, 'The text of *Miss Mackenzie*', *Nineteenth-century fiction 3* 305-8

Carleton Green, 'Trollope in Hawaii', *Nineteenth-century fiction 3* 297-303

Marcie Muir, *Anthony Trollope in Australia* (Adelaide, Wakefield Press)

Lance O. Tingay, *The Bedside Barsetshire* (London, Faber & Faber)

1950

Morton W. Bloomfield, 'Trollope's use of Canadian history in *Phineas Finn*' *Nineteenth-century fiction 5* 67-74

Bradford A. Booth, 'Trollope on the novel', in *Essays critical and historical dedicated to Lily B. Campbell* (Los Angeles, University of California Press), pp 217-31

Beatrice Curtis Brown, *Anthony Trollope* (Denver, Colorado, Alan Swallow)

David Stryker, 'The significance of Trollope's *American Senator*', *Nineteenth-century fiction 5* 141-9

Lance O. Tingay, 'Trollope's first novel', *Notes & Queries 195*, 563-4

Lance O. Tingay, 'Trollope's Library', *Notes & Queries 195* 476-8

G.M. Tracy, 'L'oeuvre de Trollope: ou le paradis perdu', *Mercure de France 308* 434-5 (March)

1951

John Draper, *Barchester Towers: a comedy in three acts* (London, John Draper). First performed on 11 February 1952 in Manchester

Russell A. Fraser, 'Anthony Trollope's younger characters', *Nineteenth-century fiction 6* 96-106

Frank E. Robbins, 'Chronology and history in Trollope's Barset and Parliamentary novels', *Nineteenth-century fiction 5* 303-16

Lance O. Tingay, 'The reception of Trollope's first novel', *Nineteenth-century fiction 6* 195-200

1952

'Akanthos', 'A Victorian novelist invests in bank shares', *The Banker's Insurance Manager's and Agent's Magazine 173* 234-36. On AT's banking investments

Asa Briggs, 'Trollope, Bagehot and the English constitution', *Cambridge Journal 5* 327-38. Reprinted in *Victorian People* (Chicago, University of Chicago Press, 1955)

Clement Franklin Robinson, 'Trollope's Jury Trials', *Nineteenth-century fiction 6* 247-68

1953

Robert M. Adams, '*Orley Farm* and real fiction', *Nineteenth-century fiction 8* 27-41

Robert H. Taylor, 'On rereading *Barchester Towers*', *Princeton University Library Chronicle 15* 10-15

1954

Clement Attlee, 'The pleasure of books' *National and English Review 142* 17-21. Includes a brief appreciation of Trollope

Louis Rocher, 'Autour de Trollope', *Etudes anglaises 7* 224-6

Wayne Schumaker, 'The mixed mode: Trollope's *Autobiography*', in *English Autobiography* (Berkeley and Los Angeles, University of California Press), pp 158-84

1955

A.O.J. Cockshut, *Anthony Trollope: a critical study* (London, Collins). Reprinted 1968 (New York, New York University Press)

Maude Houston, 'Structure and plot in *The Warden*' *University of Texas Studies in English 34* 107-13

1956

William Coyle, 'Trollope as social-anthropologist' *College English 17* 392-97

Robert A. Donovan, 'Trollope's prentice work' *Modern Philology 53* 179-86

Rafael Helling, *A century of Trollope criticism* (Helsinki, Societas Scientiarium Fennica). Reprinted 1967 (Port Washington, New York, Kennikat Press)

Rafael Koskimies, 'Novelists' thoughts about their art: Anthony Trollope and Henry James', *Neuphilologische Mitteilungen 57* 148-55

Mario Praz, 'Anthony Trollope', in *The Hero in eclipse in Victorian fiction* (London/New York, Oxford University Press), pp 261-318

Lord Schuster, *Trollope and the Law* (London, Inner Temple Library). Privately circulated

Patricia Thompson, *The Victorian Heroine: a changing ideal 1837-1873* (London OUP), passim

Lance O. Tingay, 'Trollope's popularity: a statistical approach', *Nineteenth-century fiction 11* 223-29

1957

Camilla Zauli-Naldi, 'James e Trollope', *Studi Americani 3* 205-19

1958

Bradford A. Booth, *Anthony Trollope: aspects of his life and art* (Bloomington, Indiana, Indiana University Press)

Russell A. Fraser, 'Shooting Niagara in the novels of Thackeray and Trollope', *Modern Language Quarterly 19* 141-6

Wilson B. Gragg, 'Trollope and Carlyle', *Nineteenth-century fiction 13* 266-70

John Hagan, '*The Duke's Children:* Trollope's psychological masterpiece', *Nineteenth-century fiction 13* 1-21

Arthur Mizener, 'Anthony Trollope: the Palliser novels' in *From Jane Austen to Joseph Conrad: essays collected in memory of James T. Hillhouse*, pp 25-54

1959

Sonia Bicanic, 'A missing page of *The Claverings*', *Studia Romanica et Anglica Zagrabiensia 8* 13-15 (December)

John Hagan, 'The divided mind of Anthony Trollope', *Nineteenth-century fiction 14* 1-26

1960

Sonia Bicanic, 'Some new facts about the beginning of Trollope's *Framley Parsonage*', *Studia Romanica et Anglica Zagrabiensia 9-10* 171-6

Hugh Sykes Davies, *Trollope* (London/New York for the British Council and the National Book League). No.18 in the series Writers and their Work

Hugh Sykes Davies, 'Trollope and his style', *A Review of English Literature 1* 73-85 (October)

Ramesh Mohan, 'Trollope's political novels (Chronicles of Parliamentary life)', *The Indian Journal of English Studies 1* 57-69

Jerome Thale, 'The problem of structure in Trollope', *Nineteenth-century fiction 15* 147-57

1961

Ralph Arnold, *The Whiston matter: the Reverend Robert Whiston versus the dean and chapter of Rochester* (London, Rupert Hart–Davies). On a supposed original for the plot of *The Warden*

Louis Auchincloss, 'Americans in Trollope', in his *Reflections of a Jacobite* (Boston, Houghton Mifflin), pp 113-25

G.F.A. Best, 'The road to Hiram's Hospital: a byway of early Victorian history', *Victorian Studies 5* 135-50

Thomas B. Lundeen, 'Trollope and the mid-Victorian episcopate', *Historical Magazine of the Protestant Episcopal Church 30* 55-67

1962

Bradford A. Booth, 'Author to publisher: Anthony Trollope and William Isbister', *Princeton University Library Chronicle 24* 51-67

John E. Dustin, 'Thematic alternation in Trollope', *Publications of the Modern Language Association of America 77* 280-7

Sherman Hawkins, 'Mr Harding's church music', *English Literary History 29* 202-23

Robert Bernard Martin, 'Better than ambition: the Master of St. Cross Hospital', and 'The imposthume of much wealth: George Hudson and the railway mania', in his *Enter Rumour: four early Victorian scandals* (New York, Norton), pp 137-84 and 187-241

Sabine Nathan, 'Anthony Trollope's perception of the

way we live now', *Zeitschrift für Anglistik und Amerikanistik 10* 259-78

1963

William Cadbury, 'The uses of the village: form and theme in *The Vicar of Bullhampton*', *Nineteenth-century fiction 18* 151-63

P.D. Edwards, 'Trollope changes his mind: the death of Melmotte in *The Way We Live Now*', *Nineteenth-century fiction 18* 89-91

Margaret Hewitt, 'Anthony Trollope: historian and sociologist', *British Journal of Sociology 14* 226-39

Bert G. Hornback, 'Anthony Trollope and the calendar of 1872: the chronology of *The Way We Live Now*', *Notes & Queries 208* 454-58. With an editorial note appended by J.C. Maxwell

1964

William Cadbury, 'Character and the mock heroic in *Barchester Towers*', *Texas Studies in Literature and Language 5* 509-19

V.S. Pritchett, 'Trollope was right', in his *The living novel & later appreciations* (New York, Random House), pp 128-40

W. David Shaw, 'Moral drama in Barchester Towers', *Nineteenth-century fiction 19* 45-54

Donald Smalley, 'Anthony Trollope', in *Victorian fiction: a guide to research,* ed Lionel Stevenson (Cambridge, Mass, Harvard University Press), pp 188-213. A survey of criticism of Trollope's works

1965

'Oliver Edwards' (i.e. William Haley), 'Trollope's singletons', *The Times* 25 Mar, 15

P.D. Edwards, 'Anthony Trollope's 'Australian' novels', *Southerly: a review of Australian literature 25* 200-7

Pamela Hansford Johnson, 'Anthony Trollope: an odd fish', *New York Times Book Review,* 25 Apr, 2

Blair G. Kenney 'Trollope's ideal statesman: Plantagenet Palliser and Lord John Russell', *Nineteenth-century fiction 20* 281-5

1966

David Aitken, ''A kind of felicity': some notes about Trollope's style', *Nineteenth-century fiction 20* 337-53

'Oliver Edwards' (i.e. William Haley), 'Three men in a shop', *The Times,* 20 Oct, 16. On *The Struggles of Brown, Jones and Robinson*

Edgar F. Harden, 'The alien voice: Trollope's western senator', *Texas Studies in Literature and Language 8,* 219-34

Robert M. Polhemus, '*Cousin Henry:* Trollope's notes from underground', *Nineteenth-century fiction 20* 385-9

Sheila M. Smith, 'Anthony Trollope: the novelist as a moralist', in *Renaissance and modern essays presented to Vivian de Sola Pinto,* ed G.R. Hibbard (New York, Barnes & Noble) pp 129-36

1967

J.R. Dinwiddy, 'Who's who in Trollope's political novels', *Nineteenth-century fiction 22* 31-46

Carol H. Ganzel, '*The Times* correspondent and *The Warden*', *Nineteenth-century fiction 21* 325-36

Kathleen E. Morgan, 'The relevance of Trollope', *English 16* 173-7

Robert L. Slakey, jr, 'Melmotte's death: a prism of meaning in *The Way We Live Now*', *English Literary History 34* 248-59

Tony Tanner, 'Trollope's *The Way We Live Now:* its modern significance', *Critical Quarterly 9* 256-71

1968

Ruth apRoberts, 'Trollope Empiricus', *The Victorian Newsletter 34* 1-7

M.S. Bankert, 'Newman in the shadow of *Barchester Towers*', *Renascence 20* 153-61

David S. Chamberlain, 'Unity and irony in Trollope's *Can You Forgive Her?*', *Studies in English Literature 8* 669-80

P.D. Edwards, 'Trollope and the reviewers: three notes', *Notes & Queries 213* 418-20

Arnold Goldman, 'Trollope's *North America*', *TLS* 28 Nov, 1338. See further 5 Dec, 1385, 12 Dec, 1409 and 19 Dec, 1433

Robert M. Polhemus, *The Changing World of Anthony Trollope* (Berkeley and Los Angeles, University of California Press)

Gordon N. Ray, 'Trollope at full length', *The Huntington Library Quarterly 31* 313-40

1969

Ruth apRoberts, 'Anthony Trollope, or the man with no style at all', **Victorian Newsletter 35** 10-13

Ruth apRoberts, 'Trollope's one world', *South Atlantic Quarterly 68* 463-77

J.H. Davidson, 'Anthony Trollope and the colonies', *Victorian Studies 12* 305-30

P.D. Edwards, *Anthony Trollope* (London, Routledge & Kegan Paul: Profiles in Literature series)

Louis Kronenberger, *'Barchester Towers'*, in *The Polished Surface* (New York, Knopf), pp 217-32

A.H. Reed, editor, *With Anthony Trollope in New Zealand* (Wellington, A.H. and A.W. Reed). Includes passages from Trollope's *Australia and New Zealand,* and newspaper accounts of his visit

Donald Smalley, editor, *Trollope: the critical heritage* (New York, Barnes & Noble; London, Routledge & Kegan Paul). Reprints many contemporary reviews of AT's novels

1970

Robert B. Heilman, 'Trollope's *The Warden*: structure, tone, genre', *Essays in honor of Esmond Linworth Marilla,* ed T.A. Kirby and W.J. Olive (Baton Rouge, Louisana State University Press) pp 210-29

James R. Kincaid, *'Barchester Towers and the nature of conservative comedy'*, *English Literary History 37* 595-612

John Christopher Kleis, 'Passion vs. prudence: theme and technique in Trollope's Palliser novels', *Texas Studies in Literature and Language 11*, 1405-14

Ivan Melada, 'The idea of a gentleman: *Dr Thorne'*, in his *The Captain of Industry in English fiction 1821-1871* (Albuquerque, University of New Mexico Press), pp 166-71

1971

Ruth apRoberts, *Trollope: Artist and Moralist* (London, Chatto & Windus). Published in the US as *The Moral Trollope* (Athens, Ohio, Ohio University Press)

Richard Crossman, 'The politics of Anthony Trollope', *New Statesman n.s. 82* 754-6

Alice Green Fredman, *Anthony Trollope* (New York/London, Columbia University Press, Columbia Essays on Modern Writers, no. 56)

James Gindin, 'Trollope', in *Harvest of a quiet eye: the novel of compassion* (Bloomington, Indiana, Indiana University Press), pp 28-56

Mary Hamer, 'Working diary for *The Last Chronicle of Barset'*, *TLS* 24 Dec, 1606

Hugh L. Hennedy, *Unity in Barsetshire* (The Hague/Paris, Mouton)

Pamela Hansford Johnson, 'Trollope's young women'. in *On the novel: a present for Walter Allen*, ed B.S. Benedikz (London, Dent), pp17-33

Juliet McMaster, 'The unfortunate moth: unifying theme in *The Small House at Allington'*, *Nineteenth-century fiction 26* 127-44

James Pope-Hennessy, *Anthony Trollope* (London, Jonathan Cape; Boston. Little, Brown)

C.P. Snow, 'Trollope: the psychological stream', in *On the novel: a present for Walter Allen*, ed B.S. Benedikz (London, Dent), pp 3-16

William A. West, 'Trollope's Cicero', *Mosaic 4*, iii 143-52

1972

N. John Hall, 'Trollope and Carlyle', *Nineteenth-century fiction 27* 197-205

Hugh L. Hennedy, 'Love and famine, family and country in Trollope's *Castle Richmond'*, *Eire–Ireland 7*, 4 48-66

Douglas Hewitt, 'A partnership in mediocrity: *The Way We Live Now'*, in *The approach to fiction: good and bad readings of novels* (London, Longman)

Helmut Klinger, 'Varieties of failure: the significance of Trollope's *The Prime Minister'*, *English Miscellany 23* 167-83

Norman Page, 'Trollope's conversational mode', *English Studies in Africa 15* 33-7

David Skilton, *Anthony Trollope and his contemporaries: a study in the theory and conventions of mid–Victorian fiction* (London, Longman; New York, St Martin's Press)

R.C. Terry, 'Three lost chapters of Trollope's first novel', *Nineteenth-century fiction 27* 71-80

1973

Charles Blinderman, 'The servility of dependence: the Dark Lady in Trollope', *Images of women in fiction: feminist perspectives*, ed Susan Koppelman Cornillon (Bowling Green, Ohio, Bowling Green University Popular Press), 55-67

Mary Hamer, 'Chapter divisions in early novels by Anthony Trollope', *Notes & Queries 218* 249

Mary Hamer, 'Forty Letters of Anthony Trollope', *The Yearbook of English Studies 3* 206-15

Samuel F. Pickering, jr, 'Trollope's poetics and authorial intrusion in *The Warden and Barchester Towers*', *Journal of Narrative Technique 3* 131-40

David Skilton, '*The Fixed Period:* Anthony Trollope's novel of 1980', *Studies in the literary imagination 6* 39-50

Roger L. Slakey, 'Trollope's case for moral imperative', *Nineteenth-century fiction 28* 305-20

George Watson, 'Trollope's forms of address', *Critical Quarterly 15* 219-30

E.W. Wittig, 'Significant revisions in Trollope's *The Macdermots of Ballycloran*', *Notes & Queries 218* 90-1

1974

David Aitken, 'Anthony Trollope on 'the Genus Girl'', *Nineteenth-century fiction 28* 417-34

René Elvin, 'Anthony Trollope à la BBC TV', *La nouvelle Revue des Deux Mondes* 473-4 (May)

John J. Galvin, 'Trollope's 'most natural English girl'', *Nineteenth-century fiction 28* 477-85

N. John Hall, 'An unpublished Trollope manuscript on a proposed history of World Literature', *Nineteenth-century fiction 29* 206-10

John Halperin, 'Politics, Palmerston and Trollope's Prime Minister', *Clio 3*, 187-218

Michael Hardwick, *The Osprey Guide to Anthony Trollope* (Reading, Osprey). Published in the US as *A Guide to Anthony Trollope* (New York, Scribners)

Shirley Robin Letwin, 'Trollope, the Pallisers and the way we view now', *TLS* 5 Jul, 727-8. On the televised adaptation of the Palliser novels

George Levine, 'Can you forgive him? Trollope's *Can You Forgive Her?* and the myth of realism', *Victorian Studies 18* 5-30

Juliet McMaster, ''The meanings of words and the nature of things': Trollope's *Can You Forgive Her?*' *Studies in English Literature 14* 603-18

Simon Raven, 'The writing of 'The Pallisers'', *The Listener 91* 66-8

William A. West, 'The Anonymous Trollope', *Ariel 5* 46-64 (Jan)

1975

John W. Clark, *The language and style of Anthony Trollope* (London, André Deutsch)

N. John Hall, *Salmagundi: Byron, Allegra, and the Trollope family* (Pittsburgh, Beta Phi Mu). Prints for the first time a poem by Mrs Trollope and four poems in the hand of (and perhaps by) AT

N. John Hall, 'Trollope reading aloud: an unpublished record', *Notes & Queries 220*, 117-8

Mary Hamer, '*Framley Parsonage:* Trollope's first serial', *Review of English Studies n.s. 26* 154-70

Laurence Lerner, 'Literature and money', *Essays and Studies 28* 106-22

C.P. Snow, *Trollope: his Life and Art* (London, Macmillan; New York, Scribners)

Donald D. Stone, 'Trollope, Byron, and the conventionalities', in *The Worlds of Victorian Fiction*, ed J.H. Buckley (Cambridge, Mass, Harvard University Press), pp 179-203

Stephen Wall, 'Trollope, Balzac, and the reappearing character', *Essays in Criticism 25* 123-44

1976

Joan Mandel Cohen, *Form and realism in six novels of Anthony Trollope* (The Hague, Mouton)

P.D. Edwards, 'Trollope and 'All the Year Round'', *Notes & Queries 23* 403-5

Richard H. Grossman and Andrew Wright, 'Anthony Trollope's libraries', *Nineteenth-century fiction 31* 15-25

N. John Hall, 'Trollope's commonplace book, 1835-40', *Nineteenth-century fiction 31* 15-25

Geoffrey M. Harvey, 'Scene and form: Trollope as a dramatic novelist', *Studies in English Literature* [Rice University, Texas] *16* 631-44

Geoffrey M. Harvey, 'The form of the story: *Trollope's The Last Chronicle of Barset*', *Texas Studies in Literature and Language* 18 82-97

Walter Mayforth Kendrick, 'Balzac and British realism: mid-Victorian theories of the novel', *Victorian Studies 20* 5-24

James R. Kincaid, 'Bring back 'The Trollopian'', *Nineteenth-century fiction 31* 1-14

Margaret F. King, 'Trollope's Orley Farm: chivalry versus commercialism', *Essays in Literature 3* 181-93

Anthony Laude, '*Barchester Towers*: a new source?' *Notes and Queries 23* 59-61

W.J. Overton, 'Trollope: an interior view', *Modern Language Review 71* 489-99

Donald D. Stone, 'Trollope as a short story writer', *Nineteenth-century fiction 31* 26-47

1977

Ruth apRoberts, 'Carlyle and Trollope', in *Carlyle and his contemporaries: essays in honour of Charles Richard Sanders* (Durham, NC, Duke University Press), pp 205-26

Ruth apRoberts, 'Emily and Nora and Dorothy and Priscilla and Memima and Carry', in *The Victorian experience: the novelists* (Athens, Ohio University Press), ed. Richard A. Levine, pp. 87-120

Daniel Becquemont, 'Politics in literature, 1874-1875: *The Way We Live Now* and *Beauchamp's Career*', in *Politics in literature in the nineteenth century* (Lille and Paris, Editions Universitaires), ed Pierre Coustillas, pp 135-51

George Butte, 'Ambivalence and affirmation in *The Duke's Children*', *Studies in English Literature* [Rice University, Texas] *17* 709-27

David R. Eastwood, 'Trollope and Romanticism', *Victorian Newsletter 52* 1-5

P.D. Edwards, 'Trollope's working papers as evidence of his contributions to *Saint Paul's*', *Victorian Periodicals Newsletter 10* 68-71

N. John Hall, 'Millais' illustrations for Trollope', *University of Pennsylvania Library Chronicle 42* 23-45

John Halperin, *Trollope and Politics: a study of the Pallisers and others* (London, Macmillan; New York, Barnes & Noble). Reviews: John Vincent in *Observer* 24 Jul, p. 29; A.O.J. Cockshut in *TLS* 5 Aug, p. 957; Janet Egleson Dunleavy, in *Studies in the Novel 10* 281-3; George Levine, in *Novel 11* 274-8; Patrick Seindon in *Notes & Queries 26* 354-6; R.C. Terry in *Modern Philology 77* 310-14; Valerie Shaw in *Yearbook of English Studies 10* 320-1

John Halperin, 'Trollope, James and the international theme', *Yearbook of English Studies 7* 141-7

Geoffrey M. Harvey, 'Bulwer-Lytton and the rhetorical design of Trollope's *Orley Farm*', *Ariel 6* 68-79

Francis P. Magoun, jr, 'Plantagenet Palliser toils over decimal coinage', *Neuphilologische Mitteilungen 78* 77

Alice Schreyer, ''Ignorance is not innocence': Anthony Trollope as novelist and preacher', *Columbia Library Columns* [Columbia University, New York] *26* 11-19

R.C. Terry, *Anthony Trollope: the artist in hiding* (London, Macmillan; Totawa, New Jersey, Rowman and Littlefield). Reviews: John Halperin in *Studies in the Novel 10* 366-7; Frank W. Bradbrook in *Notes & Queries 26* 356-7; Juliet McMaster in *English Studies in Canada 6* 254-7; Arthur Pollard in *Yearbook of English Studies 10* 319-20; George Levine in *Novel 14* 78-81

Judith Weissman, ''Old maids have friends': the unmarried heroine of Trollope's Barsetshire novels', *Women and Literature 5* 15-25

T.A. Zyryanova, 'Svoeobrazie realizma v romane A. Trollopa *Barchesterkie bashne*' [The originality of the realism in A. Trollope's novel *Barchester Towers*], *Problemy metoda, zhanra i stilya v progressivnoi literature Zapada XIX-XX vv. 1976* 116-30

1978

Nicolae Balota, 'Phineas Finn si cutia de posta' [Phineas Finn and the letter box], *Romania literara* [Bucharest] *11:32* 20

Harry C. Bauer, 'Anthony Trollope's serial harvest', *Serials Librarian 2* 231-9

J.D. Coates, 'Moral patterns in *The Way We Live Now*' *Durham University Journal 40* 55-65

P.D. Edwards, *Anthony Trollope: his art and scope* (St Lucia, Queensland University Press; Hassocks, Harvester Press) Reviews: Sheila M. Smith in *Review of English Studies 30* 490-1; W.D. Maxwell-Mahon in *Unisa English Studies 17:2* 59-60; Robert Tracy in *CLIO 9* 321-2

Arnold B. Fox, 'Aesthetics of the problem novel in Trollope's *Phineas Finn*', *Journal of Narrative Technique 8* 211-19

John Halperin, 'Trollope and feminism', *South Atlantic Quarterly 77* 179-88

John Halperin, 'Trollope's *Phineas Finn*', *English Studies* [Amsterdam] *59* 121-37

Christopher Herbert, 'Trollope and the fixity of self', *Publications of the Modern Language Association of America 93* 228-39

Susan L. Humphreys, 'Trollope on the sublime and beautiful', *Nineteenth-century fiction 33* 194-214

James R. Kincaid, *The novels of Anthony Trollope* (Oxford, Clarendon Press). Reviews: A.O.J. Cockshut, *TLS* 5 Aug 1977, p. 957; John Halperin in *Studies in the novel 9* 360-3; George Levine in *Novel 11* 274-8; V.S. Pritchett in *New Statesman 94* 85-6; Ruth apRoberts in *Journal of English and Germanic Philology 77* 458-61; John Halperin in *CLIO 7* 327-30; R.C. Terry in *Modern Philology 77* 310-14

William J. Overton, 'Self and society in Trollope', *English Literary History 45* 285-302

George Papancev, 'Antani Trolap i 'Semejstvo Palisar' [Anthony Trollope and 'The Pallisers'], *Narodna kultura* [Sofia], 12 May p. 4

Lowry Pei, '*The Duke's Children*: reflection and reconciliation', *Modern Language Quarterly 39* 284-302

Arthur Pollard, *Anthony Trollope* (Boston, Massachusetts, and London, Routledge and Kegan Paul). Reviews: John Halperin in *Studies in the Novel 10* 363-5; Frank W. Bradbrook in *Notes & Queries 26*

256-7; Hugh L. Hennedy in *Arnoldian 6:3* 26-30; R.C. Terry in *Modern Philology 77* 310-14; George Levine in *Novel 14* 78-80

Robert Tracy, *Trollope's later novels* (Berkeley and London, California University Press). Reviews: Sheila M. Smith in *Review of English Studies 30* 490-1; John Halperin in *Studies in the Novel 11* 123-6; Juliet Dusinberre in *Notes & Queries 26* 492; James R. Kincaid in *Journal of English and Germanic Philology 79* 259-60; George Levine in *Novel 14* 78-82

1979

Günter Burger, 'Soziographie und Märchen: Anmerkungen zu Anthony Trollopes *Doctor Thorne*', *Literatur in Wissenschaft und Unterricht 12* 163-71

Martin Crawford, '*Barchester Towers*: an allusion and a note on composition', *Notes & Queries 26* 304-5

Dalton Gross, 'Trollope's Mr Quiverful: an addendum to John W. Clark's *The Language and Style of Anthony Trollope*', *English Language Notes 17* 122-4

Geoffrey M. Harvey, 'Trollope's debt to the Renaissance drama', *Yearbook of English Studies 9* 256-69

Juliet McMaster, *Trollope's Palliser novels: theme and pattern* (London, Macmillan). Reviews: Valerie Shaw in *Yearbook of English Studies 11* 322-44; Robert M. Polhemus in *Journal of English and Germanic Philology 80* 264-7

John Charles Olmsted and Jeffrey Egan Welch, *The Reputation of Anthony Trollope: an annotated bibliography, 1925-1975* (New York and London, Garland) Review: Michael Collie in *English Studies in Canada 6* 375-8

R.H. Super, 'Trollope's *Vanity Fair*', *Journal of Narrative Technique 9* 12-20

John Sutherland, 'The fiction earning patterns of Thackeray, Dickens, George Eliot and Trollope', *Browning Institute Studies 7* 71-92

Robert H. Tener, 'The authorship of the *Spectator's Orley Farm* review', *English Language Notes 17* 34-9

1980

Tony Bareham, editor, *Anthony Trollope* (London, Vision Press). Reviews: Frank W. Bradbrook in *Notes & Queries 29* 252-3; J.P. Vernier in *Yearbook of English Studies 13* 334-6

58

J.P. Corbett, 'Two more Trollope letters', *Notes & Queries* 27 212-15

Ramona L. Denton, ''That cage' of femininity: Trollope's Lady Laura', *South Atlantic Bulletin 45:1* 1-10

N. John Hall, *Trollope and his illustrators* (London, Macmillan). Reviews: John Bayley in *Listener 105* 115-16; Frank W. Bradbrook in *Notes & Queries 29* 253-4

Geoffrey Harvey, *The Art of Anthony Trollope* (London, Weidenfeld & Nicholson)

Susan L. Humphreys, 'Order – method: Trollope learns to write', *Dickens Studies Annual 8* 251-71

John E. Khan, 'The Protean narrator, and the case of Trollope's Barsetshire novels', *Journal of Narrative Technique 10* 7-98

Walter M. Kendrick, '*The Eustace Diamonds*: the truth of Trollope's fiction', *English Literary History 46* 136-57

Walter M. Kendrick, *The Novel Machine: the theory and fiction of Anthony Trollope*. (Baltimore and London, Johns Hopkins University Press). Reviews: Lowry Pei in *Modern Language Quarterly 41* 295-8; Nancy Aycock Metz in *College Literature 8* 198-200

Shirley Robin Letwin, 'Trollope on generations without gaps', *Daedalus 107:4* 53-70

George Levine, 'Trollope Redux', *Novel 14* 78-83

Robert Tracy, 'Instant replay: Trollope's The Landleaguers, 1833' *Eire-Ireland 15* Summer, 30-46

1981

George Butte, 'Trollope's Duke of Omnium and the 'path of history': a study of the novelist's politics', *Victorian Studies 24* 209-27

David R. Eastwood, 'Romantic elements and aesthetic distance in Trollope's fiction', *Studies in Short Fiction 18* 395-405

David R. Eastwood, '*Katchen's Caprices*, Harper's Weekly, Trollope & Dickens', *American Notes & Queries 19* 76-8

Hilary Gresty, 'Millais and Trollope: author and illustrator', *Book Collector 30* 43-61

N. John Hall, 'Trollope's letters to Harriet and Mary Knower', *Princeton University Library Chronicle 43* 23-37

N. John Hall, editor, *The Trollope critics* (London, Macmillan). Reviews: George Butte in *Victorian Studies 25* 502-4; Andrew Wright in *TLS* 19 Mar, p. 322

Bertha Keveson Hertz, 'Trollope's racial bias against Disraeli', *Midwest Quarterly 22* 374-91

Naomi Jacobs, 'Of grace and grease: two oily clergymen', *Dickens Studies Newsletter 12* 47-8
Conor Johnston, 'The Macdermots of Ballycloran: Trollope as a conservative-liberal', *Eire-Ireland 16* Summer, 71-92

Margaret F. King, 'The place of Lucius Mason in Trollope's studies of perversity', *South Atlantic Bulletin 45:4* 43-54

Judith Knelman, 'Trollope's experiments with anonymity', *Victorian Periodicals Review 14* 21-4

Judith Knelman, 'Trollope's relationship to Dickens', *Dickens Studies Newsletter 12* 9-11

Coral Lansbury, *The reasonable man: Trollope's legal fiction* (Princeton and Guildford, Princeton University Press). Reviews: Andrew Wright in *TLS* 19 Mar, p. 322; Robert A. Colby in *Modern Philology 80* 94-6; George Butte in *Victorian Studies 25* 502-4; Valerie Shaw in *Modern Language Review 80:4* 915; R.H. Super in *Modern Language Studies 16:3* 336-41; Alan Shelston in *Notes & Queries 30* 361; R.D. McMaster in *Nineteenth-century fiction 36* 487-9; R.C. Terry in *Ariel 15:1* 92-5

Edwin McDowell, 'About books and authors', *New York Times Book Review* 20 Dec, p. 22

R.D. McMaster, 'Trollope and the terrible meshes of the law: *Mr Scarborough's family*', *Nineteenth-century fiction 36* 135-56

R.D. McMaster, 'Women in *The Way We Live Now*', *English Studies in Canada 7* 68-80

Nancy Aycock Metz, '*Ayala's Angel*: Trollope's late fable of change and choice', *Dickens Studies Annual 9* 217-32

Jacques Roubard, 'La prose invisible d'Anthony Trollope', *Critique 37* 166-98

Ramon Saldivar, 'Trollope's *The Warden* and the fiction of realism', *Journal of Narrative Technique 11* 166-83

1982

century fiction 37 350-7

Ruth apRoberts, ' Trollope and the *Zeitgeist*', *Nineteenth-century fiction 37* 259-71

J.W. Bailey, '*The Duke's Children*: rediscovering a Trollope manuscript', *Yale Library Gazette 57:1/2* 34-8

Richard Barickman, Susan MacDonald and Myra Stark, *Corrupt relations: Dickens, Thackeray, Trollope, Collins and the Victorian sexual system* (New York, Columbia University Press). Review: Andrew Saunders in *TLS* 25 Mar, p. 288
Sally Brown, ''This so-called autobiography'': Anthony Trollope, 1812-1882', *British Library Journal 8* 168-73

Philip Collins, 'Business and bosoms: some Trollopian concerns', *Nineteenth-century fiction 37* 293-315

Philip Collins, *Trollope's London* (Leicester, Victorian Studies Centre, University of Leicester)

K.J. Fielding, 'Trollope and the Saturday Review', *Nineteenth-century fiction 37* 430-42

John Halperin, editor, Trollope: centenary essays (London, Macmillan). Reviews: Hugh L. Hennedy in *Arnoldian 12:2* 29-30; Susan Peck MacDonald in *South Atlantic Quarterly 83* 480-1; Richard C. Burke in *Journal of English and Germanic Philology 83* 248-50; Walter Kendrick in *Nineteenth-century fiction 38* 109-11

Geoffrey Harvey, 'A parable of justice: drama and rhetoric in *Mr Scarborough's Family*', *Nineteenth-century fiction 37* 419-29

Helen Heineman, 'Anthony Trollope: the compleat traveller', *Ariel 13:1* 33-50

James R. Kincaid, 'Trollope's fictional autobiography', *Nineteenth-century fiction 37* 340-9

Elizabeth Landland, 'Society as formal protagonist: the examples of *Nostromo* and *Barchester Towers*', *Critical Inquiry 9* 359-78

Shirley Robin Letwin, *The gentleman in Trollope: individuality and moral conduct* (Cambridge, Harvard University Press, and London, Macmillan). Reviews: Roy Foster in *TLS* 25 Jun, p. 700; Peter Kemp in *Listener 107* 22 Apr, pp 22-3; Eugene Hollahan in *Studies in the Novel 15* 150-4; Peter Stansky, in *Raritan 2:4* 128-9; Valerie Sanders in *Notes & Queries 30* 543; Andrew Wright in *Nineteenth-century fiction 38* 104-9

J. Hillis Miller, 'Trollope's *Thackeray*' *Nineteenth-*

Richard Mullen, 'Like Palliser he was an advanced conservative liberal', *Listener 108* 9 Dec, pp 9-10

Ross C. Murfin, 'The gap in Trollope's fiction: The Warden as an example', *Studies in the Novel 14* 17-30

Ira Bruce Nadel, 'Trollope as biographer', *Prose Studies 5* 318-25

Jane Nardin, 'Tragedy, farce and comedy in Trollope's *He Knew He Was Right*', *Genre 15* 303-13
Bill Overton, *The unofficial Trollope* (Brighton, Harvester Press). Reviews: Susan Morgan in *Studies in the Novel 16* 354-5; R.F. Foster in *Dickensian 80* 121-2

David Pearson, ''The letter killeth': epistolary purposes and techniques in *Sir Harry Hotspur of Humblethwaite*', *Nineteenth-century fiction 37* 396-418

Robert M. Polhemus, 'Being in love in *Phineas Finn / Phineas Redux*: desire, devotion, consolation', *Nineteenth-century fiction 37* 383-95

Arthur Pollard, Trollope and the evangelicals', *Nineteenth-century fiction 37* 272-92

Michael Riffaterre, 'Trollope's metonymies', *Nineteenth-century fiction 37* 329-39

Edward Seidensticker, 'Trollope and Murasaki: impressions of an orientalist', *Nineteenth-century fiction 37* 464-71

Patricia Thomas Srebrnik, 'Trollope, James Virtue, and *Saint Paul's Magazine*', *Nineteenth-century fiction 37* 443-63

R.H. Super, 'Trollope at the Royal Literary Fund', *Nineteenth-century fiction 37* 316-28

R.H. Super, *Trollope in the Post Office* (Ann Arbor, Michigan University Press) Reviews: Charles R. Perry in *Victorian Studies 25* 504-5; Valerie Shaw in *Modern Language Review 80:4* 914; Alan Shelston in *Notes & Queries 30* 360-1; K.J. Fielding in *Modern Philology 80* 324-6; Ruth apRoberts in *Michigan Quarterly Review 23* 141-2; Andrew Wright in *Nineteenth-century fiction 38* 104-9

John A. Sutherland, 'Trollope at work on *The Way We Live Now*', *Nineteenth-century fiction 37* 472-93

Robert Tracy, ''The unnatural ruin': Trollope and nineteenth-century Irish fiction', *Nineteenth-century fiction 37* 358-82

Andrew Wright, 'Anthony Trollope: daydream and nightmare', *Essays by Divers Hands 42* 109-20

1983

Robert A. Colby, 'Trollope as Thackerayan', *Dickens Studies Annual 11* 261-77

Mary L. Daniels, *Trollope-to-reader: a topical guide to digressions in the novels of Anthony Trollope* (Westport, Connecticut, and London, Greenwood Press)
Owen Dudley Edwards, 'Anthony Trollope, the Irish writer', *Nineteenth-century fiction 38* 1-42

Karen Faulkner, 'Anthony Trollope's apprenticeship', *Nineteenth-century fiction 38* 161-88

Stanley Hauerwas, 'Constancy and forgiveness: the novel as a school for virtue', *Notre Dame English Journal 15:2* 23-54

Christopher Herbert, '*He Knew He Was Right*, Mrs Lynn Linton and the duplicities of Victorian marriage', *Texas Studies in Literature and Language 25* 448-69

John G. Hynes, 'Anthony Trollope and the Irish question', *Etudes irlandaisies 8* 212-28

Judith Knelman, 'Trollope's journalism', *Library 5* 140-55

Jerome Meckier, 'The cant of reform: Trollope rewrites Dickens in *The Warden*', *Studies in the Novel 15* 202-23

Donald D. Stone, 'Trollope studies, 1976-1981', *Dickens Studies Annual 11* 313-33

Gertrude M. White, 'Truth or consequences: the real world of Trollope's melodrama', *English Studies 64* 491-502

Andrew Wright, *Anthony Trollope: dream and art* (Chicago, Chicago University Press). Reviews: Richard C. Burke in *Journal of English and Germanic Philology 84* 381-4; Roger L. Slakey in *Arnoldian 12:2* 25-8; Richard Altick in *London Review of Books 6:8* 11-12

1984

Tony Bareham, editor, *The Barsetshire Novels: a casebook* (London Macmillan). Review: Alan Shelston in *Notes & Queries 33:1* 124

Elizabeth R. Epperly, 'Trollope's notes on drama',

Notes & Queries 31 491-7

Sarah Gilead, 'Trollope's The Small House at Allington', *Explicator 42:1* 12-14
Michael Gorra, 'The apostle of common sense', *Hudson Review 36* 765-71

N. John Hall and Nina Burgis, editors, *The letters of Anthony Trollope* (Stanford, Stanford University Press, 2 vols). Reviews: Hugh L. Hennedy in *Arnoldian 12:2* 20-4; Nolan Miller in *Antioch Review 42* 379; W. Baker in *English Studies 67:3* 277-9; R.C. Terry in *Review 8* 215-29; Juliet McMaster in *Journal of English and Germanic Philology 85:2* 282-4; Stephen Wall in *TLS* 3 Feb, p. 114; Richard Altick in *London Review of Books 6:8* 11-12

John Halperin, 'Trollope and the American Civil War', *CLIO 13* 149-55

Susan E. Hendricks, 'Henry James as adapter: *The Portrait of a Lady* and *Can You Forgive Her?*', *Rocky Mountain Review of Language and Literature 38* 35-43

Marvin Mudrick, 'The man of the feeling', *Hudson Review 36* 755-65

1985

John E. Dustin, 'A new Trollope letter', *American Notes & Queries 23* 108-9

Arnold B. Fox, 'Nightmare to daydream to art', *Review 7* 207-13

Sarah Gilead, 'Trollope's orphans and 'the power of adequate performance', *Texas Studies in Literature and Language 27* 86-105

N. John Hall, 'Editing and annotating the letters of Anthony Trollope', in *English Forum 1* (New York, AMS Press)

John Halperin, 'Trollope as letter writer', *South Atlantic Quarterly 84* 89-98

John Halperin, 'Trollope, James and the 'retribution of time'', *Southern Humanities Review 19:4* 301-8

Robert Hughes, 'Trollope and fox-hunting', *Essays in Literature 12* 75-84

Iva G. Jones, 'Patterns of estrangement in Trollope's *The Way We Live Now*' in *Amid Visions and Revisions: poetry and criticism on literature and the arts* (Baltimore, Morgan State University Press)

Anne K. Lyons, *Anthony Trollope: an annotated*

bibliography of periodical works by and about him in the United States and Great Britain to 1900 (Greenwood, Florida, Penkevill). Reviews: Judith Knelman in *Victorian Periodicals Review 18* 156-7

Francine G. Navakas, 'The case for Trollope's short stories', *Modern Philology 83:2* 172-8

Gay Sibley, 'The spectrum of 'taste' in *Barchester Towers'*, *Studies in the Novel 17* 38-52

Lance O. Tingay, *The Trollope collector: a record of writings by and books about Anthony Trollope* (London, Silverbridge Press)

Andrew Wright, 'Trollope transformed, or the disguises of Mr Harding and others', in *Victorian Literature and Society: essays presented to Richard D. Altick* (Columbus, Ohio State University Press), edited James R. Kincaid and Albert J. Kuhn pp 315-30; Arnold B. Fox in *Review 7* 207-13; Alan Shelston in *Notes & Queries 33:1* 336-41

1986

Tony Bareham, 'First and last: some notes towards a re-appraisal of Trollope's *The Macdermots of Ballycloran* and *The Landleaguers'*, *Durham University Journal 78:2* 311-17

Richard C. Burke, 'Accommodation and transcendence: last wills in Trollope's novels', *Dickens Studies Annual 15* 291-307

Elizabeth R. Epperly, 'Trollope and the young Astuin Dobson', *Victorian Periodicals Review 19:3* 90-9

Ann Frankland, '*Barchester Towers*: a study in dialetics', *Publications of the Mississippi Philological Association* 197-208

Sarah Gilead, 'Trollope's ground of meaning: *The Macdermots of Ballycloran'*, *Victorian Newsletter 69* 23-6

Sarah Gilead, 'Trollope's *Autobiography*: the strategies of self-production', *Modern Language Quarterly 47:3* 272-90

N. John Hall, 'Seeing Trollope's *Autobiography* through the press: the correspondence of William Blackwood and Henry Merivale Trollope', *Princeton University Library Chronicle 47:2* 189-223

Laura Hapke, 'He stoops to conquer: redeeming the fallen women in the fiction of Dickens, Gaskell and their contemporaries', *Victorian Newsletter 69* 16-22

Kate Browder Heberlein, 'Barbara Pym and Anthony Trollope: communities of imaginative participation',

Pacific Coast Philology 19 95-100

R. Hughes, 'Spontaneous order and the politics of Anthony Trollope', *Nineteenth-century fiction 41:1* 32-48

John Hynes, 'Anthony Trollope's creative 'culture-shock'', *Eire-Ireland 21:3* 124-31

John Hynes, 'A note on Trollope's *Landleaguers'*, *Etudes irlandaises 11* 65-70

A. Abbott Ikeler, 'That peculiar book: critics, common readers and *The Way We Live Now'*, *College Language Association Journal 30:2* 219-40

Edward H. Kelly, 'Trollope's *Barchester Towers'*, *Explicator 44:2* 28-9

Michael Lund, 'Literary pieces and whole audiences: *Denis Duval, Edwin Drood, and The Landleaguers'*, *Criticism 28:1* 27-49

R.D. McMaster, *Trollope and the law* (Basingstoke, Macmillan)

D.A. Miller, 'The novel as usual: Trollope's *Barchester Towers'*, in *Sex, Politics and Science in the nineteenth century* (Baltimore, John Hopkins University Press)

Jane Nardin, 'Comic convention in Rachael Ray', Papers on Language and Literature 22:1 39-50

Jane Nardin, 'Conservative comedy and the women of *Barchester Towers'*, *Studies in the Novel 18:4* 381-94

David Skilton, 'The Trollope reader' in *The nineteenth-century British Novel* (London, Arnold), edited Jeremy Hawthorn, pp 142-55

R.H. Super, 'A review essay: modern scholarship on the Trollopes', *Modern Language Studies 16:3* 336-41

R.C. Terry, 'Living at a gallop', *Review 8* 215-29

Robert Tracey, 'Stranger than truth: fictional autobiography and autobiographical fiction', *Dickens Studies Annual 15* 275-89

Michael Riffaterre, 'On the diegetic functions of the descriptive', *Style 20:3* 281-94

John Sutherland, 'The commercial success of The Way We Live Now: some new evidence', *Nineteenth-century fiction 40:4* 460-7

R.H. Super, 'Modern scholarship on the Trollopes', *Modern Language Studies 16:3* 336-41

Robert H. Taylor, 'Trollope's girls', *Princeton University Library Chronicle 47:2* 229-47

Yujiu Zhang, 'Random remarks on Trollope's *Autobiography*', *Foreign Literature Studies* [China] *33:3* 74-9. In Chinese

1987

Elizabeth R. Epperly, 'From the borderlands of decency: Madam Max Goesler', *Victorian Institute Journal 15* 25-35

Elizabeth R. Epperly, 'Trollope reading old drama', *English Studies in Canada 13:3* 281-303

L. Felber, 'Genre in search of an historical context: Trollope's nineteenth-century proto-roman-fleuve', *Genre 20:1* 25-43

Peter W. Graham, 'Emma's three sisters', *Arizona Quarterly 43:1* 39-52

Mary Hamer, *Writing by numbers: Trollope's serial fiction* (Cambridge, Cambridge University Press)

John G. Hynes, 'An Eye for an Eye: Anthony Trollope's Irish masterpieces', *Journal of Irish Literature 16:2* 54-8

Thomas A. Langford, 'Trollope's satire in *The Warden*', *Studies in the Novel 19:4* 435-47

Susan Peck MacDonald, *Anthony Trollope* (Boston Twayne, English Authors series)

J. Hillis Miller, *The Ethics of Reading, Kant, de Man, Eliot, Trollope, James and Benjamin* (New York, Columbia University Press)

Henry N. Rogers III, 'Trollope and James: the 'germ' within', *Studies in English Literature 27:4* 647-62

John Sutherland, 'Trollope, publishers and the truth' *Prose Studies 10:3* 239-49

R.C. Terry, editor, *Trollope: interviews and recollections* (London and New York, Macmillan)

Stephen Wall, 'Trollope, satire and *The Way We Live Now*', *Essays in Criticism 37:1* 43-61

Patricia A. Vernon, 'The poor fictionist's consequence: point of view in the Palliser novels', *Victorian Newsletter 71* 16-20

1988

Harold Bloom, editor, *Anthony Trollope's Barchester Towers and The Warden: modern critical interpretations* (New York, Chelsea)

Elizabeth R. Epperly, *Anthony Trollope's notes on the old English drama* (Victoria, British Columbia, University of Victoria Press, English Literary Studies monographs series)

John G. Hynes, '*The American Senator*: Anthony Trollope's critical chronicle of a winter at Dillsborough'' *English Studies 69* 48-54

James R. Kincaid, 'Reassessing Trollope', *TLS* p. 1395

Judith Knelman, 'Anthony Trollope: English journalist and novelist, writing about the famine in Ireland', *Eire-Ireland 23:3* 57-67

Kal Parker, 'Reassessing Trollope', *TLS* p. 1313

Mary Rosner, 'The two faces of Cicero: Trollope's life in the nineteenth century', *Rhetoric Society Quarterly 18* 251-8

David Skilton, 'The relation between illustration and text in the Victorian novel: a new perspective', in *Word and visual imagination: studies in the interaction of English literature and the visual arts* (Erlangen, Univ. Bibliothek Erlangen-Nurnberg)

Roger L. Slakey, 'Anthony Trollope: master of gradualness', *Victorian Institute Journal 16* 27-35

F. Smith, 'Reassessing Trollope', *TLS* p. 1313

R.H. Super, *The Chronicler of Barsetshire: a life of Anthony Trollope* (Ann Arbor, University of Michigan Press)

J. Thompson, 'Reassessing Trollope', *TLS* p. 1313

Lance O. Tingay, *Anthony Trollope, politician: his parliamentary candidature at Beverly, 1868* (London, Silverbridge Press)

Stephen Wall, *Trollope and character* (London, Faber, and New York, Henry Holt)

Robert Woodall, 'Anthony Trollope and the Beverly Election', *Contemporary Review 253* 320-24

1989

Arnold Craig Bell, *A Guide to Trollope* (Braunton, Devon, Merlin)

Elizabeth R. Epperly, *Patterns of repetition in*

Trollope (Washington, Catholic University of America Press)

Victoria Glendinning, 'Laundry Lists', *TLS* p. 718

J. Kucich, 'Transgression in Trollope', *English Literary History 56:3* 593-618

Paul Lyons, 'The morality of irony and unreliable narrative in Trollope's *The Warden* and *Barchester Towers*', *South Atlantic Review 54:1* 41-54

Jane Nardin, *He Knew She Was Right: the independent woman in the novels of Anthony Trollope* (Carbondale, Southern Illinois University Press)

R.C. Terry, *Trollope Chronology* (London, Macmillan)

Lance O. Tingay, *Homage to Barsetshire: a radio script* (London, Silverbridge Press). Not broadcast

Donald T. Stone, 'James, Trollope and the 'vulgar materials of tragedy'', *Henry James Review 10:2* 100-3

1990

J.L. Chevalier, 'Women and prudence in the Palliser novels', *Cahiers victoriens et edouardiens 31* 63-78

L.J. Dessner, 'The autobiographical matrix of Trollope's *The Bertrams*', *Nineteenth-century fiction 45:1* 26-58

Helen Heineman, *Three Victorians in the New World: interpretations of America in the works of Frances Trollope, Charles Dickens and Anthony Trollope* (New York, P. Lang)

Richard Mullen, *Anthony Trollope: a Victorian in his World* (London, Duckworth)

A.M. Ross, ''Ploughshares into swords': the Civil War landscape of Trollope's *North America*', *Nineteenth-century fiction 45:1* 59-72

L.J. Swingle, *Romanticism and Anthony Trollope: a study in the continuities of nineteenth-century literary thought* (Ann Arbor, University of Michigan Press)